Volunteers in Child Health:

Management
Selection
Training
&
Supervision

Arlene Barry Kiely

First Edition, 1992

With the permission of the Association for the Care of Children's Health, limited quantities of this publication have been reprinted and made available for distribution by:

Child Life Council Inc,
11821 Parklawn Drive, Suite 310
Rockville, Maryland 20852-2539
(301) 881-7090
clcstaff@childlife.org
www.childlife.org

Published by the Association for the Care of Children's Health
7910 Woodmont Avenue, Suite 300
Bethesda, MD 20814
(301) 654-6549

First Edition
First Printing
1992

ISBN 0-937821-72-1

Table of Contents

Acknowledgments v
Foreword vii

Section 1 — Administration and Management

Introduction – What Is Needed? 3

1.1 – Always Include Staff 7
　◆ Misconceptions and Answers

1.2 – Needs Assessment 11
　◆ How To Assess Your Needs for Volunteers
　◆ Coordinating Overall Agency Needs

1.3 – Is It Worth It? A Cost/Benefit Analysis 15

1.4 – Refining Job Descriptions and Selection Criteria 17

1.5 – Standardizing the Application Process 19

1.6 – Interviewing and Screening Applicants 21
　◆ How to Interview a Prospective Volunteer
　◆ Screening Red Flags ◆ Concluding the Interview
　◆ How to Say "No" Gracefully ◆ Checking References

1.7 – Recruitment 31

1.8 – Documentation of Services 33

1.9 – Recognition and Rewards 35
　◆ Ongoing Appreciation ◆ Official Recognition
　◆ Recognizing Outstanding Supervisors

1.10 – When Volunteers Leave 39

1.11 – Dismissing Volunteers 41

1.12 – Special Issues:
　Entertainers, Visitors, Holidays, and Donated Goods . . 43
　◆ Is it Appropriate? ◆ Visitors ◆ Holidays ◆ Donated Goods

Section 2 — Orientation and Training

Introduction — Why Taking Time Saves Time 51
　◆ What Kind of Orientation? ◆ What About Small Programs?
　◆ You Can Succeed, One Step at a Time

2.1 – Introduction to the Agency, Job Description,
　　and Environment 53
　◆ Introducing the Job Description and Environment

2.2 – Orientation to the Volunteer Role 57
- Ways to Explore the Role

2.3 – Helping Volunteers Develop Realistic Expectations . . . 61
- What Do Volunteers Want? - Sharing Common Fears
- Taking a Realistic Look at Fears

2.4 – Policies and Procedures 67

2.5 – Special Considerations in Health Facilities 69
- Safety - Infection Control - Confidentiality and Privacy

2.6 – Information and Skills for Working with
Children and Families 71
- The Impact of Health Care Experiences - Child Development - Supporting Normal Development and Coping Through Play - Books and Expressive Arts - Communication Skills
- Age-Appropriate Preparation for Health Care Experiences
- Self-Reflection and Sharing Significant Observations

Section 3 — The Art of Supervision

Introduction 79

3.1 – What Is Supervision? 81

3.2 – Why Supervise? 83

3.3 – Barriers to Supervision 85

3.4 – Communicating Expectations 89
- Supervisor's Preferences - Other Considerations

3.5 – Assessment 93

3.6 – Understanding Your Preferences 95

3.7 – The Individual Supervisory Plan 99
- Guidelines for Planning Individual Supervision

3.8 – Promoting Volunteers 103

3.9 – Improving Performance: Coaching vs. Criticism 105

3.10 – Practicing Supervision: Eight Opportunities 107
- Group Instructions for Supervisory Opportunities
- Role-Play Observers' Worksheet

3.11 – Conclusion: Supervisory Skills Review and Action Plan . . 129
- What Good Supervisors Do
- Supervisory Development Action Plan

Appendix A — Administrative Resources A1

Appendix B — Orientation and Training Resources B1

Appendix C — Evaluation of Publication C1

Acknowledgments

Authors understand why Academy Awards recipients have trouble limiting the list of those who deserve thanks for their achievement. While this publication does not feature a cast of thousands, the theme song of acknowledgements could well be the Beatles' refrain, "I get by with a little help from my friends."

My teachers and fellow students include many coworkers and volunteers at Children's National Medical Center in Washington, DC. By sharing our gifts and learning from our mistakes, we learned together the principles of human resource management that form the basis of this manual.

Each ACCH member who reviewed this manual brought special skills to the task. Pat Johnson added clarity and refinement throughout the document. Susan Murray not only reviewed but provided invaluable editorial assistance from start to finish. Susan Kolodner shared her management expertise. Robert Quinn generously added excellent resources. Katrina Weader, Maggie Loftus, and Robyn Fell added practical suggestions. The many ACCH staff members who lent their enthusiasm, creativity and expertise, also deserve a round of applause.

All of us thank Beverley Johnson, first Executive Director of ACCH, who recognized the need for this publication and had the vision to pursue it. Her leadership and commitment continue to inspire and direct advocacy efforts at all levels of health care.

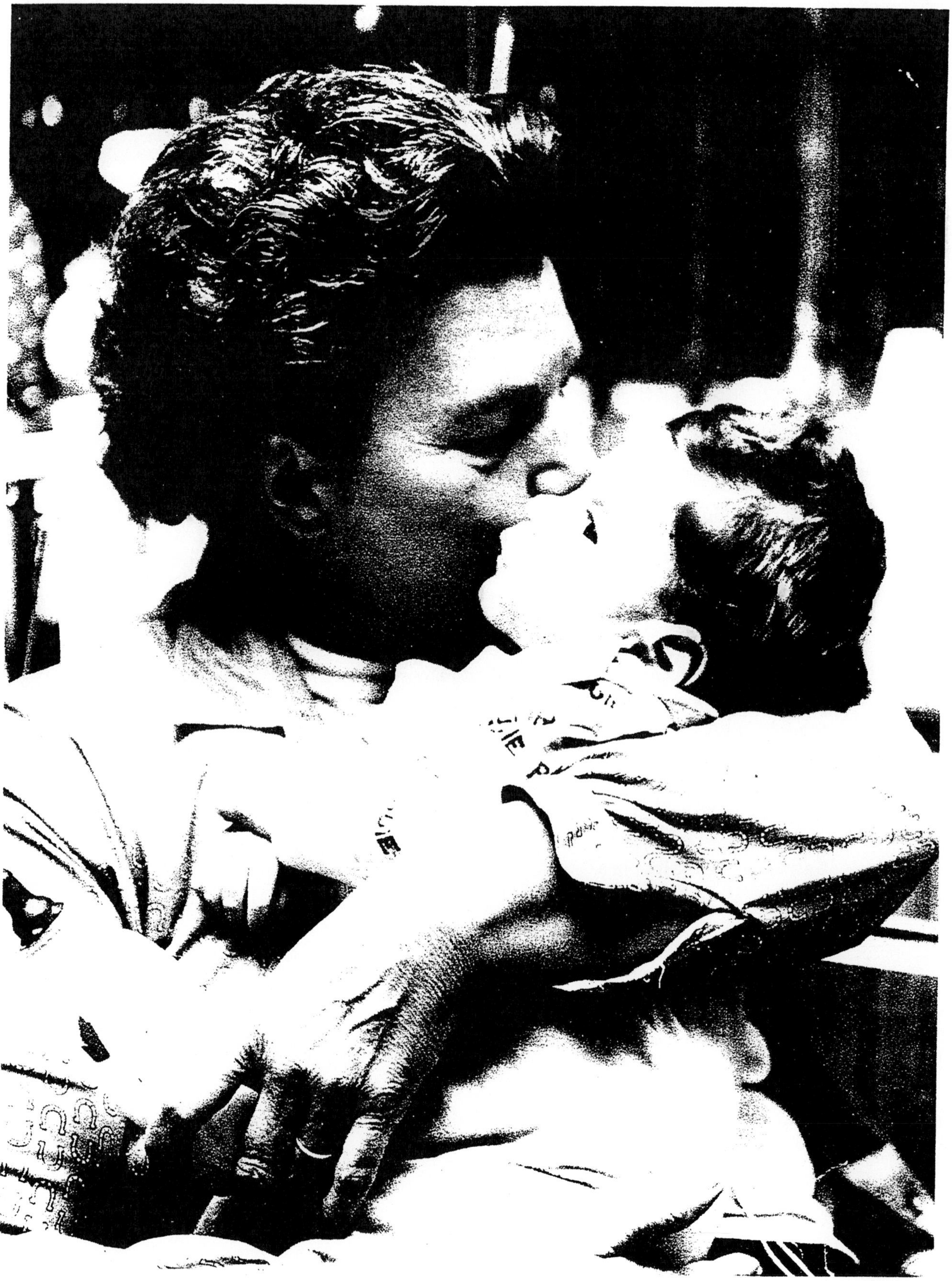

Foreword

VOLUNTEERING IS A TIME-HONORED TRADITION in child health and welfare. For generations, in all kinds of communities, people have supported friends and neighbors in times of need. As society became more complex, much historic child health and welfare reform was initiated by public-spirited women. Altruism rooted in spiritual or humanitarian conviction has been a prime motivator of much volunteer service. Whatever the origin, the tradition of volunteering is alive and well. Despite the increasing commitment to work, family, and schooling, a majority of North Americans regularly volunteer their time and talents. Volunteering in support of child and family health remains a favored choice for women, men, youth, and elders from all backgrounds.

We are fortunate to live in a culture where volunteer service is a valued tradition, for volunteers are needed more than ever. In today's complex society, family life is increasingly precarious. Substance abuse, domestic violence, poverty, homelessness, inadequate or unaffordable health care, lack of affordable housing, the rising cost of living, the increase in single-parent families, and the feminization of poverty all threaten family stability. More and more, children and families need the support of health care agencies; volunteers play vital roles in providing this support.

There are meaningful roles for volunteers in the full range of health care services for children — ambulatory clinics, hospitals, emergency rooms, home care agencies, school health programs, and day care centers, to mention a few. Increasingly, there are children with chronic illnesses and long-term disabilities who interact frequently with the health care system and to whom consistent volunteers can offer support. In addition, new health education efforts for wellness and disease prevention are being developed, and volunteers can play an important role in these endeavors.

In facing contemporary challenges, there are no substitutes for the care, commitment, and skill of creative human beings. How can we best make use of the invaluable gifts volunteers bring? How can we ensure that these irreplaceable human resources are not squandered, diverted, or discouraged by poor management? How can we make certain that volunteers who work with children and families have appropriate skills, supervision, and support?

This publication is offered to explain and support those practices that are vital in the management, selection, training, supervision, retention, and recognition of child health volunteers. We are grateful to the many ACCH members throughout the United States and Canada who have generously shared their thoughts and their training materials. This multidisciplinary sharing, which is the hallmark of ACCH, will continue to enrich the lives of the children and families we serve.

Section 1

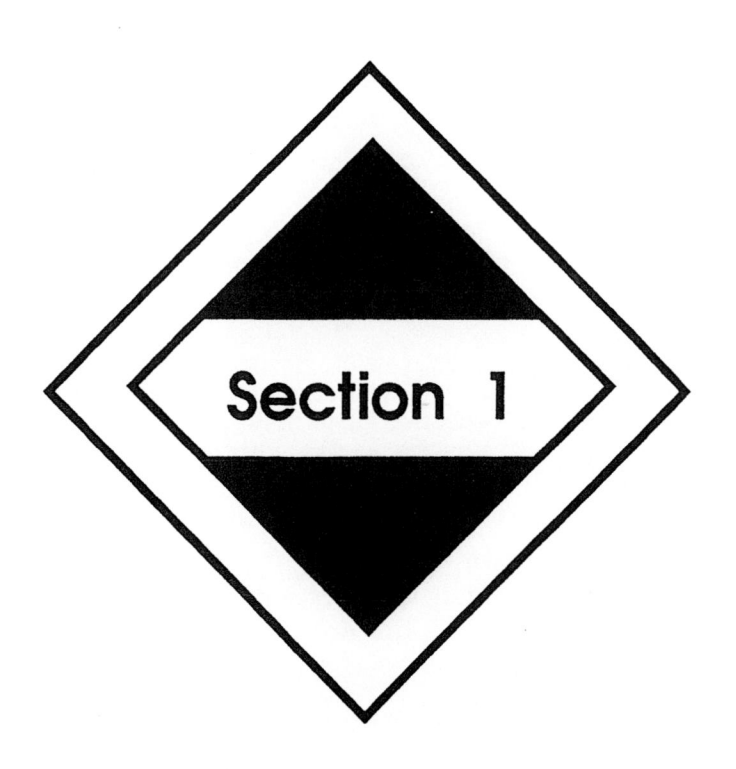

Section 1

Administration and Management

Table of Contents

Introduction – What Is Needed?	3
1.1 – Always Include Staff	7
◆ Misconceptions and Answers	
1.2 – Needs Assessment	11
◆ How To Assess Your Needs for Volunteers	
◆ Coordinating Overall Agency Needs	
1.3 – Is It Worth It? A Cost/Benefit Analysis	15
1.4 – Refining Job Descriptions and Selection Criteria	17
1.5 – Standardizing the Application Process	19
1.6 – Interviewing and Screening Applicants	21
◆ How to Interview a Prospective Volunteer	
◆ Screening Red Flags ◆ Concluding the Interview	
◆ How to Say "No" Gracefully ◆ Checking References	
1.7 – Recruitment	31
1.8 – Documentation of Services	33
1.9 – Recognition and Rewards	35
◆ Ongoing Appreciation ◆ Official Recognition	
◆ Recognizing Outstanding Supervisors	
1.10 – When Volunteers Leave	39
1.11 – Dismissing Volunteers	41
1.12 – Special Issues: Entertainers, Visitors, Holidays, and Donated Goods	43
◆ Is it Appropriate? ◆ Visitors ◆ Holidays ◆ Donated Goods	

Introduction

What Is Needed?

WHEN YOU WERE A CHILD, did you enjoy looking at those drawings that challenged you to examine, "What is wrong with this picture?" This same approach is helpful in analyzing the differences between effective and ineffective volunteer programs. For example, do any of these comments sound familiar?

- *"Volunteers come for a few times and just fade away...."*
- *"No one tells me when to expect a volunteer, so I can never get ready."*
- *"They keep sending me volunteers whether or not I have asked for them."*
- *"Volunteers don't seem to know what to do."*
- *"I don't have time to train and supervise volunteers and provide the services children need as well."*

Obviously, something is wrong in the many agencies where these complaints are heard. Everyone wants an effective volunteer program, recognizing that an unsatisfactory volunteer experience is bad for the volunteer, the staff, and possibly for the agency's reputation. It *is* possible to prevent the revolving door syndrome. First we must ask, "What's wrong with this picture?"

Effective volunteer programs are those that meet the needs of everyone involved: the agency, staff members, clients, and volunteers. Programs that are based on defined needs, careful selection, training, and supervision, and have a clear management structure result in satisfaction for volunteers and staff alike.

A good program does not happen by goodwill alone. Each agency must have a qualified person with responsibility and authority for the volunteer program. All good programs require needs assessment, screening, selection, orientation and training, supervision, and rewarding of volunteers. This is the only way to assure equal opportunity and selection based on matching individual applicant qualifications with overall agency needs. Ideally, this is done by a paid director of volunteer services. However, in small agencies a staff member can be designated, provided this individual is qualified in all aspects of personnel management and understands the special qualifications required of volunteers for pediatric services. (Some department managers in sensitive areas, such as child protection clinics or child life services, prefer to interview and select final volunteer candidates for these sensitive positions.)

What is Needed?

The Agency Needs

A volunteer coordinator who
- is qualified in every aspect of personnel management and program planning
- is responsible for needs assessment, administrative procedures, and coordination of the agency's overall volunteer services
- understands the special qualifications for child health volunteers
- knows how to implement the ten essential steps for successful volunteer programs

Staff Members Need

- opportunity to define the kind of help they need
- freedom to decline a proposed service
- time to plan and arrange work for a volunteer
- time to orient and welcome a volunteer
- dependable volunteers
- training in effective supervision

Volunteers Need

- meaningful work, worth their time and effort
- a clear job description
- thorough orientation
- training in the do's and don'ts
- a capable and willing supervisor
- opportunity to give and get feedback
- appreciation, recognition, rewards

Clearly designated responsibility and authority for volunteers is needed regardless of the size of the agency or volunteer program. In small agencies, it is tempting to assume that volunteers can be managed informally, on a case-by-case basis, and with little "bureaucracy" or organization. Because volunteers are, in reality, unpaid personnel, their management and supervision are just as important as that of paid staff members. And because each volunteer's "reimbursement" for service is different, the needs for a clear management structure and thoughtful supervision are critical to ensure the satisfaction of everyone involved. The administrative structure does not have to be bureaucratic — but it does have to exist and be based on proven standards.

What Is Needed?

The designated manager must not only have the standard knowledge, skills, and abilities required for human resource management, but must also have full authority to make decisions. Given the logistics required to coordinate a corps of many part-time volunteers, excellence in personnel and program management is more essential than commonly recognized. Regardless of the size of the agency, or of the volunteer program, the same steps to success are applicable.

Ten Essential Steps for a Successful Volunteer Program:

1. Include staff members in planning and in the decision making process.
2. Plan a program based on careful analysis of needs.
3. Calculate in advance the ratio of program cost to the benefits expected.
4. Write well-defined job descriptions for each volunteer position.
5. Establish selection criteria and a standardized application process.
6. Assure careful screening of all applicants.
7. Write performance standards for volunteers and staff supervisors.
8. Design an orientation and training program based on defined needs.
9. Teach staff how to supervise effectively.
10. Plan for on-going recognition and support.

This manual organizes the ten essential steps to success in volunteer management into three sections. Orientation and training is frequently viewed as the greatest need in pediatric volunteer management. Sound orientation is essential, but it is not the first step.

Section One of the manual outlines the first essential: How to *analyze*, *prevent*, and *correct* the most common mistakes in volunteer program planning and management. Section Two gives guidelines for staff who orient and train volunteers. Section Three is a curriculum for developing supervisory skills in staff directly responsible for individual volunteers. Administrative resources are included in Appendix A. Training materials that can be photocopied for volunteers are included in Appendix B.

Obviously, no single manual can meet the needs unique to each setting. However, the elements basic to most pediatric health care settings are included. By following the ten essential steps to success, using the materials for staff as well as those for volunteers, you will be able to develop not only a program but also a manual that meets the needs of your agency. Training for human services is dynamic, requiring the highest levels of creativity and flexibility. Our wish is for this publication to provide both a navigational chart and an anchor. The voyage is yours.

Test Yourself

Volunteer Services — True or False?
- Volunteers are needed everywhere.
- Volunteers can fill in wherever needed throughout the agency at any time.
- Any interested person should be accepted as a volunteer.
- Staff members will be grateful for any volunteer help they can get.
- Staff members can find a way to use volunteers at any time.
- It is bad public relations to turn down potential volunteers.
- Staff members should make use of certain volunteers just for public relations.
- Volunteers can learn everything they need to know on the job.
- All staff members know how to supervise and support volunteers.

All of these assumptions are false.

Chapter 1.1

Always Include Staff

THE FIRST RULE OF SUCCESS is: *Always include staff in all phases of planning and decision making.* The commitment and competence of staff of your hospital or agency is the key to the success or failure of any program. There is no substitute for the experienced perspective of staff. *Yet, front-line staff are too often the most undervalued planning resource an agency has.* While attempting to provide leadership, too many administrators, supervisors, and even volunteer coordinators can unwittingly generate failure by making false assumptions for and about the staff who are expected to benefit directly from volunteer support.

As indicated, some of the more common fallacies include:

- assuming the staff needs volunteers;
- expecting staff to be grateful for any kind of help they can get;
- expecting staff to make use of certain people just for public relations purposes;
- expecting staff to find a way to use any volunteer sent to them at any time; and
- assuming staff knows how to supervise and support volunteers.

Likewise, common fallacies about prospective volunteers are:

- it is bad public relations to screen and turn down potential volunteers;
- any interested person should be accepted;
- volunteers can just fill in wherever needed; and
- volunteers can learn everything they need to know on the job.

One of the ongoing challenges in volunteer services management is to explain the rationale for human resource standards in volunteer management, and to clarify common misconceptions about the role of volunteers. How does a volunteer coordinator, or a staff member, counteract the most common misconceptions about volunteer management? Let's review the most common misconceptions one at a time, and how each may be addressed.

Section One

Misconceptions and Answers

"We can't afford to turn volunteers away."

Do we accept every potential employee who applies? Why not? We need to be equally thoughtful in being sure volunteers are qualified to do the job. It is sometimes necessary to refer applicants elsewhere.

"If we turn people away, it is bad public relations."

In fact, the best volunteer programs have high standards and become well respected for excellence. The best potential volunteers seek a well organized program, worthy of their time and talents.

"Anyone who shows an interest ought to be able to work with children."

A good screening process is essential to select those people who have the emotional maturity, the skills, and the aptitudes to work successfully with children and families. The first responsibility is to protect children and families from inappropriate people or services.

"Volunteers should be able to learn everything they need to know on the job."

All volunteers who work with children and families in health care settings need training in child development, the impact of illness or special needs on children and families, age-appropriate play, safety, and confidentiality. Institutions can be liable for mishaps that occur due to inadequate training. Training needs to be balanced with direct experience, observations, and discussion. It takes time and planning, but pays off in volunteer commitment and appropriate service.

"Staff members ought to be glad for any help they can get any time."

In fact, having unexpected volunteers is a disruption. It prevents staff from planning a proper welcome, or preparing an assignment. Personnel are taken away from other duties. Volunteers feel awkward and not needed. This kind of situation frustrates everyone. It tells volunteers that the agency does not consider their contributions important enough to plan in advance. It makes personnel feel that their real needs are not taken seriously and that their expertise, skills, and input are not valued.

"Anyone should be able to supervise a willing volunteer."

Supervision is a learned art. All people deserve time set aside to plan, evaluate, learn, and practice supervisory skills. The time spent in planning and improving supervision is an excellent investment. It results in improved performance of volunteers, better delegation of responsibility, expansion of services, job satisfaction, and retention of staff and volunteers alike.

In summary, the coordinator must know how to counteract misconceptions to accomplish each of the ten steps needed for success. A wise manager will never forget that the foundational step is to include staff in all phases of the program, from needs assessment, to defining job descriptions, to ongoing program evaluation, to planning for recognition and rewards.

Section One

10

Volunteers in Child Health:

Chapter 1.2

Needs Assessment

IN SETTINGS THAT ARE TRADITIONALLY budget conscious, the "free" help of a volunteer is often considered too good to pass up. When this is the underlying philosophy of volunteer management, many agencies unwittingly let the needs of the volunteers determine the volunteer program, instead of asking themselves, "What kinds of help do we need?" Volunteer help may, in fact, be too valuable to pass up — but only if that assistance is meeting the agency needs as well as the volunteer's. The way to determine this is through needs assessment.

Key Questions to Ask in Needs Assessment

1. What are our specific needs for additional help?
2. Can a volunteer do those things? If not, can volunteers do some things our paid staff members currently do and free staff for other responsibilities?
3. What skills and characteristics would a volunteer need to fill these roles?
4. What will it cost us for volunteers to fill these roles?

The goal of needs assessment is to determine what kind of volunteer help is needed, by whom, where, and at what times. The answers to these questions will guide you in all other aspects of your program — recruitment, selection, training, supervision, and evaluation. The steps for doing a needs assessment are the same for a small clinic or a large hospital — the scale may be different, but the steps are the same. The specifics of "how-to" are covered in the next section of this chapter. Only when you have done a needs assessment can you make realistic plans and time lines for a volunteer program.

How To Assess Your Needs for Volunteers

THE INSPIRATION FOR A NEW VOLUNTEER service can originate over coffee, from overworked staff members, from a mother who wants someone to hold her baby while she talks to the doctor, or from a management consultant. Regardless of where the idea begins, the designated volunteer manager needs to coordinate a needs assessment. And before the needs assessment begins, the staff members who will be working with the volunteers, or who are expected to benefit from the volunteers' help, must be incorporated into the process. Many good ideas fail because well-meaning

Section One

people ignore the first rule of success and fail to consult those directly involved.

The following steps outline a helpful process for needs assessment. The goal is to determine what kind of help is needed, by whom, where, and at what times.

♦ Brainstorm

Individually, or in a small group, brainstorm answers to the questions:

- *What are our needs for additional help?*
- *What could volunteers do that would be helpful in this office, clinic, unit?*

List at least three specific services that would be helpful, such as assisting with playroom activities, feeding children, transporting children to clinics, providing activities for brothers and sisters of patients, clerical help with a public education campaign, or help with promotions. Do not evaluate any suggestion at this point ... just list as many as people can think of. By allowing spontaneity in this brainstorming process, some subtle needs and creative uses of volunteer services may emerge.

An additional step may be useful here if the volunteers will be directly serving children and families. Invite a small group of parents or children to go through the same process. Ask them: "How could volunteers help you?" Be careful, however, about raising expectations or making promises you can't keep.

♦ Evaluate and Prioritize

This step brings you back to the world of reality. Look at the list of needs that was generated and outline those that are the most important. Then go back and select the roles that are the most appropriate for volunteers. If some of your high priority needs are currently performed by staff members, evaluate whether some functions could be reassigned appropriately to a volunteer in order to free a staff member to meet the other needs. For example, a walk-in clinic recognized that it had long lines at the initial assessment and check-in stage. By using a volunteer instead of a nurse to greet clients and help them fill out the initial paperwork, the waiting time was decreased for families and the nursing staff had more time for longer interactions with the parents and children.

This is a critical step for involving the direct-line employees as well as the clients (if it is a direct-service position). The priorities of the management may be different from the priorities of the staff members. By asking the front-line people to take part in setting the priorities, you are ensuring that real needs are being met and that the employees will support the program by welcoming volunteers as team members. Likewise, if your proposed service involves clients, ask them if the service would be helpful to them.

Needs Assessment

♦ Develop Preliminary Job Descriptions

Group together any helping functions that might be performed by the same volunteer. For example, on an infant unit in a hospital a volunteer might hold babies, rock them to sleep, feed them, play with them, dress them, take them for a walk in their strollers, talk to a mother while she feeds her baby, and pick up and clean toys used by the children. Likewise, a volunteer in a well-baby clinic might greet parents, show them where they can put their coats, complete their forms for them (or offer to hold the child while they complete the forms), offer to play with other children while they are in the examination area, offer to warm bottles, and show them the diaper changing area. A volunteer in another clinic might answer telephones, schedule appointments, help with filing, and serve as the receptionist for both staff members and clients.

This initial grouping of tasks is the beginning of a job description. It can be further developed by asking, "What are the peak times of need for each of these volunteer services?" For example, if help with feeding is needed only for half an hour each morning, is this job alone worth the trip for a volunteer? What other specific duties could this same volunteer perform on an ongoing basis?

Before going any further, it is important to step back and look at what you've done so far. Does this preliminary job description look interesting? (If the job description only includes those things that everyone hates to do, you may not find people clamoring to give their time to do it!) Is the assortment of duties realistic for a volunteer to do? (If the job duties are essential, what will you do when the volunteer cannot come? You may have written a job description for a new employee . . . not a volunteer!) Are there people with the skills and interests you have described available at the times you need?

If you already have volunteers serving in your agency, involve them in helping you to answer some of these questions. They can tell you whether or not it looks workable, interesting, realistic, and rewarding.

Coordinating Overall Agency Needs

IF THE AGENCY IS SMALL and you are only planning for one volunteer to do one job, you can skip now to Chapter 1.3. But in most agencies, there are ongoing needs for many volunteers to perform different services at different times with different supervisors. A key volunteer management function then becomes the scheduling and administrative coordination of all volunteers. The following steps can help:

♦ One — Get the Big Picture

Create a visual picture of the agency's overall needs for all the volunteer services required. On a weekly calendar grid, chart the peak days and hours of need for each role. "All the time" is too vague an answer. (In a large agency, such as a hospital, a separate calendar grid may be needed for each unit or service area.)

♦ Two — How Many?

Determine and chart the ideal maximum number of qualified volunteers needed for each position in each time frame. (For example: three playroom volunteers, Wednesday, 9:00 a.m. to 12:00 noon; one tutor, Monday, 1:00 to 4:00 p.m.) Make sure there is enough work for the volunteer to do within each time frame. For each volunteer position, add the total weekly number of volunteers desired. Then add the grand total for all positions. This is the realistic picture of the ideal number of volunteers your agency can reasonably manage. *Don't* overestimate a maximum! Aim for quality, not quantity. This prevents volunteers dropping out because actual needs were overestimated.

♦ Three — Plan Monthly and Yearly Schedule

In charting the overall needs, make a yearly "guesstimate," paying attention to seasonal variations. For example, are more or fewer volunteers needed during the holidays? Are there different program needs in the summer or winter? Should you expect seasonal variations in availability of volunteers, such as more college students but fewer parents of school children available in summer? Will winter weather restrict participation by foster grandparents? Schedules for recruitment, selection, and orientation must be planned according to seasonal time lines. Make a time line by working backwards, according to the reasonable time needed for recruitment, application, selection, and training for each position.

Chapter 1.3
Is It Worth It?
A Cost/Benefit Analysis

IT IS IMPORTANT TO RECOGNIZE that although volunteers are not paid, their services are not free of cost. Ideally, volunteers extend the services of paid staff and free them for other responsibilities. However, some investment of staff time is required to insure volunteer competence. How, then, do you calculate in advance the cost/benefit ratio between the amount of staff oversight required and volunteer service you expect to receive? How much staff time will be required to make volunteer service worthwhile? The goal is to make sure that any planned volunteer service benefits more than it costs!

The bottom line of the cost/benefit calculation is to determine the minimum hours of total service per volunteer that will justify the necessary time investment of staff.

The cost/benefit analysis involves more than calculating the financial costs of a volunteer program. You must also consider such issues as:

- How many total hours must a volunteer serve in order to benefit the agency?

- How much staff time will be required to recruit, screen, orient, train, and supervise each volunteer? Can we realistically make that time available for staff?

- How long will it take before a volunteer can be expected to serve without close supervision?

- How often will it be practical to orient and supervise new volunteers? Given the amount of time it takes to orient and supervise new volunteers, are there times of the week, month, or year, that are better than others to do this?

The answers to these questions help determine your agency's policies on such things as minimal service requirements for volunteers. For example, if it takes six weeks and 20 hours of staff time to train a volunteer to do a complex task, it would not be beneficial to accept a volunteer for that position if the volunteer could only serve for two hours a week for two months, a total of 16 hours. Neither the volunteer nor the agency would derive much benefit from such a placement.

Obviously, the level of complexity of each volunteer assignment is an important orientation and supervision variable, in terms of staff time required, and needs to be considered in a cost/benefit analysis. Minimal service requirements can be adapted accordingly. For example, volunteers performing simple clerical tasks might be trained on the job, following a general orientation to the agency. However, a proven standard for volunteers working directly with children and families in a health care setting is to require a minimum of two or three hours a day, on the same day each week, for a total commitment of 100 service hours per year. Similarly, 80 service hours concentrated in a 4-week period may be deemed worthwhile. For on-going needs of any kind, a service period of less than two hours at one time is usually not even worth a volunteer's travel time. Nor does it allow enough time for the volunteer to become comfortable and feel invested in the setting or clients.

Establishing a minimum commitment requirement for volunteer service does more than justify your financial commitment. It also communicates that volunteer service is valuable. And it saves time in the application, screening, and selection process by eliminating in advance those individuals who cannot meet the minimum commitment and thus would not bring sufficient benefit to the agency.

Calculating a Cost/Benefit Ratio

1. If the volunteer job were a paid job, what would you have to pay? Compute an hourly wage (ask your human resources department to help you). Add 25% to the base wage cost to cover the benefits you would include for an employee. Then, multiply this hourly wage times the number of hours per week for a projected weekly salary. Then multiply the weekly salary by how many weeks you realistically expect the volunteer to serve. This is your projected benefit of service to the agency.

2. How many staff hours will be required to recruit, screen, train, and supervise this volunteer? Multiply the number of hours by the average hourly salary of the personnel doing the work. Add the direct cost of any benefits you give the volunteer — parking, free meal, uniforms. This is the cost of the volunteer services.

3. Divide the benefit (answer to Number 1) by the cost (answer to Number 2). If the number is one or greater, your financial benefits are greater than your expenses. You must still ask, is it worth it?

4. This simple analysis does not take into consideration the costs and cost-savings of such aspects as improved community relationships, good public relations, and improved service delivery. These "intangibles" can offset some of the financial expenses. Comfort, caring, and support to families cannot be measured in dollars.

Chapter 1.4

Refining Job Descriptions and Selection Criteria

ONCE YOU KNOW THAT A PARTICULAR volunteer job is beneficial to the agency, it is time to refine the job description and set selection criteria for volunteers who will fill that role. The initial work has been done in defining the preliminary job description. The job functions now need to be organized and made more specific. Staff who will be directly involved in supervision of volunteers need to own this process, as it clarifies their expectations of volunteers and the scope of their supervisory responsibilities.

Begin this process by asking each potential staff supervisor to list specifics for the job description. Use a separate blank sheet of paper, or photocopy the sample work sheet, Appendix A, page A2, for each potential volunteer job description. Staff should write answers — "always, sometimes, never" — to the question, "What do you expect the volunteer working with you to do?" In each category, staff should list as many specific functions as possible. The "always" category answers the question, "What specific things do I want this volunteer to do every day of assignment? Examples include: 1) Report promptly to supervisor for assignment; 2) Help prepare materials and supplies for playroom activity. The "sometimes" category lists those duties which may be infrequent or optional, such as, 1) May transport children within the agency if requested by staff; or 2) May have the option to work with children in isolation. The "never" category must clearly outline those behaviors that must be avoided at all times. These may include: 1) Will not adjust or regulate medical equipment of any kind; 2) Will not have access to patient's charts; or 3) Will refrain from giving medical advice.

From the answers to these questions, staff members will become aware of broad areas of concern, such as safety and confidentiality, that must be addressed in orientation and training. It may be sufficient, then, to state in the job description the expectation that the volunteer will "Keep the environment safe at all times," *provided* that the details of what this means is spelled out and learning is verified in training. On the other hand, certain procedural expectations, such as "Report promptly to supervisor for assignment" or "Assist in the care, cleaning, and maintenance of play equipment and supplies," might be included in a job description as a performance standard reminder.

> ## Why Write a Volunteer Job Description?
> - to clarify what is needed and expected;
> - to define the limitations of the volunteer role;
> - to guide orientation and supervision; and
> - to document the understanding between agency and volunteer.

THE SECOND STEP IN WRITING JOB DESCRIPTIONS is to ask yourself what skills or characteristics a person needs in order to do the job you have outlined. For example, consider the specialized skills and characteristics needed in each of the following situations:

- a volunteer working the cash register in a children's hospital gift shop;
- a volunteer teaching parenting skills to new adoptive parents of children with special health needs;
- a volunteer playing with children in a well-baby clinic waiting room;
- a volunteer playing with children in the burn unit of a hospital; and
- a volunteer at a camp for children with special needs.

Each of these roles has different qualifications that must be spelled out in the job description. This helps the manager of the volunteer program — whether that person be the director of volunteer services, the human resources manager, or the nursing director — recruit, select, and train the best person to meet specific needs. From these discussions, a formal, written description can be developed. (See sample, Appendix A, page A3.)

Resist the temptation to skip this participatory process by simply adapting the sample job description. Something important and unique to your setting might be missing from any sample description. This exercise helps staff think through the complexities of needs and expectations in the real situation. It brings to consciousness the performance assumptions that must be communicated to prospective volunteers in your particular setting.

As the sample indicates, a job description also gives a position title; spells out qualifications, supervision, days, hours, and location of service; and lists agency requirements such as health screening. All this information is a prerequisite to determining qualifications and making final selections. A professional director of volunteer services or the director of human resources can help the volunteer manager or other staff members develop the format and specific wording for a job description.

Chapter 1.5: Standardizing the Application Process

A STANDARDIZED APPLICATION PROCESS streamlines the screening and selection of volunteers. It will weed out impulsive applicants in advance. Good prospects appreciate standards that demonstrate the agency's respect for the contributions of volunteers. *Regardless of referral source, all candidates should follow the same equal opportunity process. Placement must never be promised in advance of application. The designated volunteer coordinator must have final selection authority.*

Sometimes, with the best of intentions, agency staff, board members, or others who feel close ties to the agency may be tempted to promise volunteer placement to specific individuals. This risks being interpreted as favoritism, and circumvention of an equal opportunity process. It undermines the volunteer coordinator's authority and responsibility. A consistent process need not prevent anyone from serving as a referral or recruitment source. It does, however, protect everyone from any expectations of favors or influence. It also gives prospective volunteers the opportunity to have a more complete picture of the variety of service options available.

Agency policy should require all prospective volunteers, as well as all staff who desire volunteers, to follow established procedures. These basic procedures have proven successful:

- All prospective applicants, regardless of referral source, should receive an application form (see sample, Appendix A, page A5) and letter or brochure describing the agency and volunteer opportunities. This eliminates needless telephone explanations, and serves to give prospects a realistic picture of needs and requirements in advance. Statistics show that approximately one-third of inquirers actually return applications.

- Receipt of applications should be acknowledged with a post card, requesting the applicant to call and schedule an interview appointment.

- A prescheduled interview should be required of all applicants. *Do not interview drop-in prospects.* An applicant's ability to follow through is a measure of commitment. An applicant who expects special treatment or immediate placement may not be willing to comply with other program standards.

Established procedures protect staff members from pressures to make exceptions, and also conserve time, energy, costs, and the agency's reputation for fairness and quality.

Chapter 1.6

Interviewing and Screening Applicants

HOW DOES AN INTERVIEWER SELECT the best qualified candidates? Interviewing involves more than matching qualified applicants with available openings. It must include screening as an essential component of risk management. Screening is the key to prevention. Inappropriate candidates must be tactfully rejected for the protection of children, parents, staff, and the agency. Therefore, the interviewer must assess each candidate's motivation, commitment, general emotional stability, and overall appropriateness for working with children and families.

Let's acknowledge that there is no fool-proof method to accomplish this. Observation, intuition, instinct, and "gut" reactions are all relied upon. All are important. All may be wrong! Nevertheless, an agency charged with the care of children must exercise every precaution in selecting volunteers. It is wiser to be wrong and reject an applicant, than to ignore reservations that could prove to be accurate predictors of poor or inappropriate performance. In short, interviewers must *pay attention to reservations about any applicant.* Skilled interviewers learn to refine their observations.

THE FIRST RULE OF INTERVIEWING is "Know thyself!" No human being can be free of subjective judgment. It is important to be aware of one's own bias and prejudice and how these influence judgment. For example, an interviewer who has a family member who is hearing-impaired may be especially pro-active when interviewing deaf people. Similarly, an interviewer might have immediate favorable response to a New England accent, simply because it reminds the interviewer of a favorite friend. Unconscious negative reactions can be even more influential. Examine your idiosyncrasies and admit to yourself the kinds and types of people who may bring forth an automatic negative *or* positive response. Work to keep these factors from unduly influencing your final judgment. Interviewers must be able to relate graciously to all kinds of people, be scrupulous in upholding equal opportunity standards, and keep an open mind while refining observations.

Experienced interviewers learn to be detectives about their gut reactions. You must bring to conscious awareness the specific sensory stimulus which evoked your reaction. Only then can you determine the significance of your reaction. Ask yourself, "Exactly what was happening when I felt this reaction?" Pinpoint as many specific behavioral observations as possible. Noting that someone "appears very nervous" is not specific enough. More precise analysis should reveal specific observations such as "sat tensely forward in chair throughout the interview," "kept clenching and unclenching hands," "eyes darted about room repeatedly," "burst into laughter at several inappropriate points," "walked with quick, jerky steps," "interrupted interviewer repeatedly." Would you be comfortable placing the individual just described in a volunteer position to work with children and families who may be highly stressed? Probably not! You don't know the cause of these behaviors, but you have observed enough specifics to raise some appropriate cautions. Behaviors that make the interviewer have reservations will probably cause the same disquiet in staff, children, and families.

Special Qualifications for Volunteers in Child Health Settings

- Primary motivation is to be supportive of children, families, and staff members.
- Appreciation for the special needs of children and families in health care settings.
- Respect for individual and family differences in style, temperament, culture, religion, beliefs, child-rearing practices, and values.
- Warmth, patience, tact, maturity, and good judgement.
- Ability to establish comfortable relationships with children and families.
- Flexibility and the ability to adapt to changing needs and conditions.
- Recognition and support for the parent as the constant in a child's life.
- Respect for confidentiality and privacy.
- Understanding of the limitations of the volunteer role, and the need for agency policies and procedures.
- Understanding the importance of taking direction from staff members and of seeking help when needed.
- Realistic expectations of the volunteer role and their own strengths and weaknesses.
- Ability to communicate questions or reservations about the volunteer experience.
- Dependability — the ability to make and keep a service commitment.

On rare occasions, you may decide to accept for a probationary period an applicant whose behaviors seem borderline, "too close to call." Many agencies require all final candidates to undergo a specified probationary period, consistent with standard employment practice. This provides a graceful out for both parties, if needed. Some candidates who at first seem borderline prove to be outstanding volunteers. Others prove unsatisfactory, and their service must be gracefully terminated.

Interviewing and Screening Applicants

Because health care experiences are stressful, children and families need support from stable, mature, and competent staff and volunteers. Thus, interviewers seek volunteers who have the qualities most needed in health care.

Happily, there will be applicants who seem to have outstanding qualifications and make a strong positive impression from the beginning. If you consider such candidates appropriate for highly sensitive areas, such as intensive care, hospice work, or child protective services, do check references to confirm your judgment. Strong, positive first impressions can be erroneous. It is important to analyze positive impressions as carefully as negative ones. Some agencies require volunteers to serve for a period in a less critical or complex area before they are eligible for high intensity service.

Note: It is not wise to waive orientation and training requirements for any volunteer, no matter how well qualified.

Standard practices are a safeguard against errors. Outstanding candidates are also needed to enrich the orientation experience of other volunteers.

How to Interview a Prospective Volunteer

INTERVIEWING IS BOTH A SKILL that can be learned, and an art that is continually challenging. The following recommendations should be helpful for interviewing potential child health volunteers.

Preparation. Prepare for every interview by briefly reviewing the application and getting an overall feel for the applicant. (Be prepared to be wrong.) Attend to what is included and to what is omitted as well. Omissions may indicate carelessness, or that something is being concealed. Application sloppiness, undue pressure of a pen, crossed out marks, may signal tension of some kind. (Or, that the cat jumped onto the applicant's paper — nevertheless, pay attention!) Make a mental note of any information, omissions, or questions you wish to pursue.

Sample Questions to Ask in an Interview

- What do you think children need from volunteers?
- What appeals to you about volunteering here?
- How do you feel about working with people who are different from you?
- Do you have any concerns about volunteering here?
- What are some things which might make the health care experience difficult for children? For families?
- How can volunteers best help parents here?
- What do you think might be some important rules and regulations for volunteers here?
- How do you think volunteers can best help staff?
- What do you hope to accomplish here? What do you feel you have to offer?
- What will you do if volunteering here is not what you expected?

Management, Selection, Training & Supervision

Privacy. All interviews should be conducted in private with no third party present. (An exception might be for a sign-language interpreter or a translator.) Each applicant's ability to function independently is something that must be assessed. Tactfully ask parents, counselors, board members, or others to wait outside. Alone with the applicant you may learn that volunteering is someone else's idea! This is not the best motivation for volunteering.

Establish rapport. Take time to establish rapport, be friendly and welcoming. Do not rush, allow interruptions or distractions. Whatever the outcome, you wish the applicant's continued goodwill toward the agency. You can begin with an open-ended remark such as, "Tell me a little bit about yourself," or "How did you happen to become interested in this agency?" or "What do you imagine yourself doing as a volunteer here?" You are trying to get a general idea of interest, purpose, and motivation.

People/children skills. Other important questions include: "Tell me about your experiences with children or with helping other people." "What have you enjoyed most?". . . "What was hardest?"

Past history often guides expectations and may be a predictor of capabilities. Remember that many people with no experience with children can make excellent volunteers. Questions such as, "Have you thought about what it would be like working with sick children (or, the children here)?" invites the applicant to express expectations, as well as reservations. Some reservations are entirely appropriate, and may be a good indicator of an applicant's openness and willingness to seek help and to learn. Excessive fears, however, may signal a need to direct the applicant to other settings for volunteering.

Dependability. Dependability is an essential requirement. Ask: "What kind of time do you have available to volunteer?" Individuals with uncertain schedules should be encouraged to wait until consistent service is possible. Resist the temptations to make exceptions! The minimum commitment is a basic requirement, no matter how well qualified an applicant seems.

Tour. If at all feasible, include a brief tour of the proposed work site. Chatting while walking puts most applicants at ease, and allows a different setting for your observations. Pay attention to signs of discomfort, over-enthusiasm, respect for confidentiality, inappropriate approaches to children or families. Invite reactions by asking afterwards, "Well, what do you think?" or "What thoughts do you have now?"

Screening Red Flags

THIS MANUAL DOESN'T ATTEMPT to teach all aspects of interviewing, but rather to point out some useful guidelines. Certain behaviors should serve as warning signals when making a final selection. These include:

An inordinate need to be of service. This may be expressed as an intense desire to begin immediately, excessive availability, or a willingness to come at any and all hours. Too much available time may indicate an inordinate personal need that the agency cannot be expected to fill.

Intense enthusiasm for children, particularly when expressed as "love for all children." Children, and adults, aren't always lovable! A realistic perspective about human reactions and interactions is desired. Frequently, self-proclaimed "lovers of children" are seeking to compensate for some lack in their own lives. Furthermore, people who see themselves as "rescuers" of "helpless" children may have difficulty respecting and supporting the parents' role as primary caregivers. In most situations, volunteers must be able to confine their services to the defined needs, and are trained not to establish permanent relationships. In those situations where long-term relationships with children are needed, it is especially important that volunteers' emotional reactions be monitored, and that only the most stable, mature, and dependable candidates are selected.

Rigidity, intolerance, or inflexibility. Openness to varieties of temperament, respect for cultural differences, empathy, and a non-judgmental attitude are important qualities for volunteers. For example, an authoritarian, no-nonsense adult might be unable to adapt to a program that encourages children to make choices about their activities.

Expressions of religious zeal. Many outstanding volunteers are motivated by religious faith. However, individuals whose agenda is to proselytize should be referred to religious organizations. A nonsectarian agency must ensure respect for all beliefs (including atheism), by protecting clients' spiritual privacy.

Recent family history of loss. Individuals who have successfully coped with loss frequently make ideal volunteers. However, it is also possible that personal grief prompts certain individuals to volunteer in health care settings. Most hospice programs require volunteers to be 13 months beyond an experience of personal loss, in order to allow sufficient time for individual grief work. In exploring past losses, general questions — such as, "What was it like?" "What was hardest?" "What helped you get through it?" — help indicate coping style and current status. What you wish to avoid are volunteers who may project their own experiences and reactions onto children and families.

Academic or professional expectations. Clarify in advance the needs and expectations of career-oriented prospects. Does an applicant expect to watch surgery most of the time? Engage in counseling? Diagnose psychological needs? Write a book? None of these agendas is appropriate for the volunteer role. The parameters of the volunteer role and confidentiality must be spelled out. Individuals qualified to practice a profession must be cautioned against doing so while serving as a volunteer. *Bona fide* professional internships should not be confused with volunteer service, but handled as educational contracts with appropriate professional supervision.

Is the applicant really looking for a job? Some agencies do hire individuals who are outstanding volunteers. This is the exception, not the rule. Qualified applicants who are first in need of immediate employment should be encouraged to re-apply for volunteer service after they have found a job elsewhere, and know how much time they can commit to volunteering.

Any need for immediate placement. Applicants who need to fulfill service requirements of a third agency, such as a school or court, must first be qualified to meet the actual needs, requirements, standards, and procedures of your agency. The needs of your agency take precedence. You should not be obligated to place any applicant from another agency unless all qualifications are met. Resist any pressure for immediate placement. The best candidates will usually explore many service options, indicating self respect for what they have to offer.

Concluding the Interview

SOME CANDIDATES WILL BE BETTER SUITED for a volunteer role not directly serving children. The interviewer should explain the position for which the individual seems especially suited. For example, "The Information Desk is one of our most difficult and important service areas. You have had so much experience dealing with the public, and seem very calm. You seem best qualified for this opening." Many such areas of high public relations contact have far reaching impact on the child's and family's sense of welcome and being cared for.

Where there are many different opportunities for volunteers, some interviewers begin by asking, "Were you interested in working directly with children or in one of the other service areas?" Similarly, the application form can also ask individuals to check their interests from a range of possibilities. Some agencies have a photo book of volunteers in action and a brief description of services for perusal by applicants who arrive early for an appointment.

At the conclusion of each interview and tour, the interviewer should review the volunteer's role and agency's expectations, explore and correct any misconceptions, and make a decision to accept or reject the applicant. For accepted candidates, final placement is chosen, and follow-up steps, such as health requirements and orientation schedule are set. Health forms should be consistent with local requirements, and received no later than the date of orientation. Many institutions provide required TB testing and rubella titre or vaccine free of charge in appreciation for volunteer commitment. Other benefits should be discussed, and might include free or discounted parking, uniforms, access to agency in-service education, discounted meal tickets, and reference letters. Service should begin immediately after orientation.

How to Say "No" Gracefully

SCREENING OUT INAPPROPRIATE CANDIDATES is a painful but essential process. The interviewer has an obligation to protect the agency and preserve the applicant's goodwill simultaneously. Success in accomplishing both these objectives may be the only reward for the delicate skill required.

The interviewer's final authority to accept or reject applicants must be supported by the agency administration and respected by staff. Even the most experienced interviewers will occasionally make selection errors, but their authority must not be undermined.

Acceptances are based on:

- volunteer job descriptions and qualifications;
- available openings;
- ability to meet time commitments; and
- applicant appropriateness for role.

In screening, many interviewers also rely on the observations of others. For example, experienced receptionists accustomed to interacting daily with many people frequently make astute quick assessments of applicants' general instability, or of exceptional graciousness and warmth. When any two staff persons share the same reactions, these should be heeded, especially if the reactions suggest caution. In rare instances, benefit-of-the-doubt interviews with a second staff person can be done, but should not be necessary. Second interviews are not cost-effective.

Final selection should be based on qualifications. Applicants who cannot meet the minimum service commitment should be deferred. When there are reservations about an applicant's motivation or stability, these *must* be heeded but *never* stated as the reason for rejection.

HOW, THEN, DOES AN INTERVIEWER tactfully screen out inappropriate candidates? Remember that the first objective is to preserve the applicant's self esteem. Therefore, *always* state the decision in terms of the agency's programs, needs, and available volunteer placements and *never* in terms of the applicant's personal deficiencies. Be cordial and appreciative of the applicant's interest. State the decision briefly and matter-of-factly; avoid being defensive or overly apologetic.

One way to begin is to state that the agency has many qualified applicants, but a limited number of openings for volunteers. You may be able to mention the agency's preference for some experiential qualification the applicant lacks, without reflecting on the applicant's personal worth. You may graciously state some (but not all) of the following as they apply to the individual:

- We have a limited number of openings . . . Only a certain number are selected for each program . . . We accept only as many volunteers as staff can supervise, and must restrict the total number of people interacting with children and their families.

- We must select the best qualified among many applicants . . . We give priority to those with a great deal of experience with children . . . prefer volunteers experienced with sick children . . . We prefer previous experience in health care settings, give priority to students in related professional education programs.

You can say that you appreciate the applicant's interest, and regret you are unable to make a match for the reasons stated. You can state that the agency needs many kinds of support, and encourages alternative service, if such is available. "I wonder if you could help us with . . . fund raising, providing safe toys or play equipment, sponsoring refreshments for a monthly birthday party, providing needed handcrafts, such as hand-knit infant layettes?" By welcoming alternative support, you communicate appreciation and frequently enlist enthusiastic support. Consider having staff brainstorm in advance a list of genuinely needed support alternatives that do not require on-site service and direct contact with children and families. *Do not*, however, offer alternative service to any candidates who prompt serious reservations. *Do not* imply that placement may be possible at some future time.

Do not, under any circumstances, be persuaded to state the subjective reasons for rejecting an applicant. Stick to programmatic explanations. Always keep decisions confidential and *do not be persuaded to discuss* with third parties. Discussions with anyone other than your direct administrative supervisor may backfire! In rare instances, an unstable individual may chose to protest the decision, thus confirming the interviewer's reasons for caution. Handle any such instance courteously and matter-of-factly. Administration should support, in advance, the decisions of the designated interviewer. It is helpful to remember that a small percentage of unstable or inappropriate applicants is to be expected, and this underlines the necessity for having a skilled interviewer and careful screening process.

Remember that no agency is obligated to accept volunteer applicants. Since volunteers are not paid, applicants cannot claim denial of opportunity for employment. Of course, legitimate equal opportunity application standards must be upheld for all candidates. Any disqualification based on race, sex, religion, national origin, or handicapping condition has no place in a health care agency.

Checking References

HOW IMPORTANT ARE REFERENCES? It is important for employers to check references for paid personnel to verify basic competence, work history, and satisfactory work habits. However, a sound screening process should eliminate the need to check references on most volunteers. Do ask for three references on the application form. You can decide whether or not to use them. Recognize that reference checks are time consuming, costly, and not always reliable. You may decide to check general references to assist a final decision for an applicant who appears borderline, or an outstanding applicant being considered for a highly sensitive area.

Few volunteer roles require a reference verification of technical competence. The agency orientation should provide the knowledge and skills required for good performance. Should you need to check references, an easy-to-complete return form or telephone call are the least costly, most efficient, and bring the best results. Many individuals hesitate to put negative information in writing. The same guidelines can be used for either method.

Interviewing and Screening Applicants

Agencies concerned about criminal record checks should realize that they may have limited value. Some agencies ask for details of felony convictions or crimes involving children.

Jurisdictional documentation and procedures for criminal record checks vary. All require the applicant's consent, and some areas require notarized consent for release of information. In an age of mobility, how does an agency decide how far back, or how far away to check? Even an FBI Fingerprint check, which some states require of family day care providers, is not fool proof. Careful screening, thorough orientation, a probationary period, and close supervision are considered more reliable safeguards.

Guidelines for Reference Checks

(Name) has applied to volunteer with children and their families at _(Agency)_. Your name was given as a reference.

How long have you known the applicant?
- In what capacity?

How would you rate his/her:
- ability to work with sick children and their families in a health care setting?
- dependability?
- calmness?
- flexibility?
- tact and confidentiality?

Is there anything else we should know before making an assignment?

Chapter 1.7 Recruitment

WHILE RECRUITMENT TAKES PLACE before interviewing, it cannot take place until the agency has defined job descriptions and standardized the application process. We have thus held discussion of recruitment until now.

Recruitment of volunteers should be targeted to meet the general needs identified for the agency and for those specific services defined by job descriptions. The realistic number of volunteers needed overall, and for each position, determines the recruitment goal. Once a program is well established, active volunteers are the best recruitment source.

Meanwhile, flyers, public service announcements, or invitations to an agency open house can be targeted to college and professional students, retirees, working people, senior citizens, service clubs, volunteer organizations, and other appropriate groups. Graduate programs in child development, psychology, social work, and special education frequently are excellent sources of volunteers, especially during summer breaks. Undergraduates can be outstanding volunteers, provided they have already learned how to balance priorities and not over commit their time and drop out during exam periods. There are also many mature and highly motivated high school students. However, it is particularly important that all assignments for youth be appropriate to experience and maturity. Exposing youth to sensitive situations, such as children with critical conditions, may result in a sense of failure rather than accomplishment. For this reason, many agencies set an entry level age requirement of 15 years, or completion of tenth grade, and restrict youth service to support areas not directly involving children who are sick.

Recruitment efforts should make clear that a standard application process will be followed, and that final selections are based on qualifications, the ability to meet minimum commitment requirements, and available openings. The myth that any willing individual should be accepted (and acceptable) ignores that both skill and commitment are required to serve children and families effectively. All child health care agencies must protect children and families from inappropriate individuals and services. The goal of the recruitment and application process is not only to select the best qualified candidates, but to accept no more volunteers than can be genuinely useful and appropriately supervised. (Many recruitment brochures also include alternative ways interested persons can support the program.)

Documentation of Services

THE TIME SPENT BY VOLUNTEERS is invaluable. It is important to record volunteer service hours for several reasons: to monitor the overall program benefits, demonstrate the value of service hours to the agency, and to reward volunteers for their cumulative contributions.

The individual volunteer's time sheet (see sample, Appendix A, page A6) provides an annual record of the hours served by day, month, and year. These sheets can be kept alphabetically in a notebook at a central locker room, volunteer office, or sign-in location. Large agencies may also use an additional daily sign-in sheet to indicate which volunteers are present on a given day. When volunteers leave the program, total service hours can be recorded on a small card for reference. Agencies vary in the length of time such records are kept, ranging from three to ten years.

Some agencies make an annual calculation of total hours served by all volunteers, and translate this figure into the full-time employment equivalent hours. For example, a full-time employee works 2,080 hours annually. Dividing this number into the total hours served annually by all volunteers gives the FTE (full-time equivalent) of all volunteer service contributed to the agency. Another calculation can reflect an appropriate dollar value of volunteer service hours. Multiply the total volunteer service hours by an average hourly wage for a monetary approximation of contributed service.

Many agencies ask regular contributors of handcrafted items (such as knit layettes for infants, bedside toy bags, hand puppets, or toys) to submit an annual record of their service hours, as well as an estimate of the monetary value of their contributions, and include these contributors in annual recognition events.

Obviously, it is not possible to calculate the intangible benefits gained from volunteer services. The value of expanding programs, assisting staff, comforting children, supporting families, preventing psychological stress, and maintaining standards of excellence and community goodwill cannot be calculated in hours or dollars. It is, nevertheless, essential that the services of volunteers be recognized, publicized, and rewarded.

Section One

Chapter 1.9

Recognition and Rewards

Ongoing Appreciation

"THANK YOU" SHOULD BE ONE OF the most frequent expressions a supervisor uses. There is no substitute for immediate appreciation for a job well done. This can be as simple as "Thanks for coming today." Or, "I look forward to Tuesdays because I know I can count on your help with the children." It may be as simple as, "Because you were here I was able to get a lot of other things done." Noting specific good work and reinforcing it immediately with praise results in continued high performance and retention. "You did a wonderful job of encouraging each of the children to paint in their own way." Or, "You were so sensitive to that child's shyness in joining the group." Or, "You moved right in and redirected that child before things got out of hand." No official recognition will be as warmly received by volunteers as the direct, immediate appreciation from colleagues on the job. Staff members who work with volunteers may need encouragement to routinely express simple and appropriate thanks to volunteers. When this habit is cultivated, employees frequently begin to express appreciation to each other with gratifying results.

Official Recognition

IT IS ALSO IMPORTANT to have a means for official recognition and appreciation for volunteer services. This need not be elaborate, but it should be done at least annually, as an expression of the agency's appreciation for all active volunteers. Although many agencies highlight National Volunteer Week each spring, you can declare your own Volunteer Day or Week at any time.

The purposes of an official celebration are: to celebrate the services of all volunteers; to express formal appreciation on behalf of the agency; to involve as many staff as possible in the celebration; and to publicize volunteers' contributions within the agency and community.

A memo to individual supervisors and areas where volunteers serve can offer suggestions of ways to honor the volunteers who work with them. A card, small gift, balloon, flowers, photo display, gift certificate, tickets to special events, or a luncheon are appropriate examples. Planning a surprise appreciation is a pleasurable activity for staff.

In addition, the annual formal agency celebration can be a single event, such as a luncheon or banquet, or involve week-long activities. Many agencies select a volunteer appreciation theme, which is highlighted throughout the agency during Volunteer Week. Examples of previous Volunteer Week themes used at the Children's National Medical Center in Washington, D.C., include: "Volunteers Are Real Lifesavers," "Volunteers Are Worth Their Weight in Gold," "Volunteers Are All Stars (mock Academy Awards)," "Volunteers Are Champs (a sports theme)," "Join the Volunteer Party (in an election year)," and "Volunteers Give Their Hearts."

A theme can stimulate creative ideas for publicity, decoration, small token favors for volunteers, theme buttons, and entertainment performed by staff. Local talent, such as a high school band or a celebrity, are frequently willing to help. Local business, corporate, or service groups may be interested in underwriting expenses for volunteer recognition for agencies that do not have a budget for special events. Most large agencies budget annually for volunteer recognition, in acknowledgement of the invaluable benefits volunteers bring to the agency.

Individual recognition can be in the form of certificates of appreciation, pins, plaques, or awards acknowledging specific numbers of hours or years of service, names added to volunteer honor rolls, and special awards for outstanding service. A planned system of recognition based on measurable service achievements, such as hours or years of service, can minimize any suggestion of competition. *It is also important that the annual celebration appropriately honor all volunteers active in the past year, whether or not a certificate or specific award has been earned.* In a well planned celebration, volunteers will experience camaraderie and pride in their collective accomplishments. Staff and volunteers alike become informed and inspired by the overall contributions of volunteers.

Agencies with little or no awards budget have frequently been creative in developing humorous, symbolic token awards, recognizing any special hardships overcome, unique job circumstances, or contributions of individual volunteers. The spirit of celebration and appreciation is far more important than formal words or expensive acknowledgements.

Some agencies surprise volunteers by displaying large celebration banners, mounting photo displays in a prominent place, or featuring volunteers in the agency or local newspaper. All such activities promote good will of volunteers, staff, and community alike.

Recognizing Outstanding Supervisors

ENCOURAGING AND REWARDING good supervisors is as important as encouraging and rewarding volunteers. This can take many forms. Noting and commenting immediately on an effective job inspires even better performance. Writing a note of personal commendation and placing a copy in the individual's personnel file is greatly appreciated. Salary increases should be considered for excellent supervisors, in recognition that their skill strengthens the program. Many agencies send a small token of appreciation to every supervisor of volunteers at least once a year.

Consistent outstanding supervision of many volunteers over a long period of time may merit special recognition. This can be as simple as a surprise bouquet of flowers during Volunteer Week, or a certificate of merit, or an outstanding supervisor award. This can serve to highlight the contributions of volunteers and supervisors as well. These awards may be most effective when presented only occasionally, and not as a matter of annual routine.

Chapter 1.10

When Volunteers Leave

EVEN THE BEST VOLUNTEERS will not stay forever. Many volunteers do not know how to say goodbye gracefully and feel guilty about leaving. Staff should be attentive to changing needs, and be supportive when volunteers decide to move on. When a volunteer moves on, three things need attention. The first is to express appreciation for the volunteer's service. This can be verbal, a letter of appreciation from the agency administrator, a small token gift, or a certificate of total service hours. A second activity is to get the volunteer's evaluation of the experience. This can be in the form of a conversation, a questionnaire, or an exit interview. (See Appendix A, page A10.) The final activity is to include a brief note on the volunteer's record of total time served, areas served, and a brief description evaluating the individual's service. Volunteers frequently will list the agency as a reference, and this information should be available in concise form.

Don't allow volunteers to fade away without appropriate appreciation to give closure to the experience. Volunteers who have had a rewarding experience will be invaluable supporters of the agency and its mission for many years to come.

Section One

Chapter 1.11

Dismissing Volunteers

THERE ARE SOME CIRCUMSTANCES that warrant the dismissal of a volunteer from the program. Attention to careful selection, orientation, and supervision of volunteers will greatly reduce the necessity for dismissals. However, even in the best of programs, the need for dismissal may arise. The overall success of a volunteer program requires a protocol for dismissal when the occasion warrants, with clearly designated responsibility and authority for dismissals.

Many agencies state directly in the volunteer policy: "At any time, the Director of Volunteer Services may dismiss a volunteer for failure to comply with agency regulations." (See, Sample Policies and Procedures, Appendix A, page A8.) Other agencies include a statement of certain grounds for dismissal, such as breach of confidentiality, in an agreement signed by each volunteer before beginning service.

Dismissals are serious, but they need not be confrontational. Careful selection and a lengthy orientation and/or probationary period provide the opportunity to gently dismiss individuals who appear to lack either the emotional stability or the supportive approaches required for work with children and families. For example, one volunteer who had responded well in the selection interview later burst into tears when she became overwhelmed by two infants who were crying simultaneously. The Director of Volunteer Services took the volunteer aside and learned that she was undergoing a divorce. "This is not the right time for you to volunteer. You are a very sensitive person. You must drop out and take care of your own needs and find the best support available for you during this time of stress." The dismissed volunteer was grateful; her self-worth preserved.

ANOTHER EXAMPLE: Some exceedingly task-oriented volunteers have been persuaded that their talents are more appropriate for tutoring in volunteer programs geared toward specific, measurable results. Play programs that promote a child's free choice of activity and require active listening skills are not always the best opportunity for many result-oriented individuals. The dismissal can be explained in terms of making the best possible match for agency and volunteer alike. Again, the volunteer's self-esteem is preserved.

However, what happens when coaching (as described in Chapter 3.10) fails to produce the desired results? What happens when volunteers commit serious errors? The general rules of personnel management apply to volunteers as well. It is important to explain in advance the behaviors that are required of volunteers. This is first spelled out in the job description and in orientation. When coaching individual volunteers for the purpose of correcting behaviors, *document what was discussed* and the date. Give the volunteer a second chance, an opportunity to correct the behavior. Depending on the seriousness of the behavior, you may issue a warning about dismissal and *document* that a warning was issued. If the behavior persists, dismissal is in order.

Any situation that involves breach of confidentiality, neglecting or harming a child, volunteering while under the influence of alcohol or drugs, or behaving in grossly inappropriate ways should be considered grounds for immediate dismissal. (It is worth noting that some volunteers dismissed for substance abuse have been successfully referred to rehabilitation programs by skilled supervisors.) However, protecting children, families, staff members, and the agency is the first obligation.

When dismissal is warranted, avoid prolonged discussion, defensiveness, or argument. Review the facts, state the reason for dismissal clearly in terms of program standards, and conclude the discussion. Document the dismissal review and date. In the most serious situations, it is wise to inform your direct supervisor of the action taken. *Remember, personnel information is confidential and should not be shared with third parties.*

Special Issues: Entertainers, Visitors, Holidays, and Donated Goods

Chapter 1.12

IT IS NOT ALWAYS EASY TO CHANNEL public interest appropriately when the interest is in "doing something for children." This is especially true regarding offers for entertainment, visiting, holiday celebrations, and donated items. These four recurring issues require special advance attention in child health care agencies. Well-managed entertainment and appropriate donations can be very beneficial. Problems arise when they are not controlled in advance.

The following five general questions should guide decisions regarding proposed services and goods:

- Is it appropriate for children and families in this setting?
- Is it safe?
- Will children, families, and staff benefit?
- How much staff time will be required to assure that things go well? Is it worth it?
- What advance planning and guidelines will simultaneously maintain goodwill, protect children and families, and preserve staff energies?

Prevention is the safeguard for all these issues. It is important that a staff person who understands the developmental needs of children and the point of view of families guide policies governing these issues. In many large agencies, a director of child life, a developmental psychologist, or a vice president for human ecology is charged with assuring that special protocols exist to protect children and families, and that all policies and procedures of the agency are evaluated in terms of developmental appropriateness, individual needs of children and families, and the need to preserve confidentiality and privacy. Experienced administrators and directors of public relations, marketing, and development welcome guidance from these experts, recognizing that it serves the overall reputation, mission, and future of the agency. Having careful guidelines and protocols established in advance eliminates being caught off guard by special requests, and enables a response that educates potential benefactors about the kinds of support that are welcomed. Written policies should designate the staff member to whom specific requests should be channeled. This individual can determine whether or not the proposed service is beneficial and appropriate, arrange a schedule for approved events, and designate a guide or manager for each event.

Is it Appropriate?

MANY SERVICES AND GOODS that are entirely suitable in a home or community setting are not advisable in settings that care for children who are sick. Children and families are more vulnerable to all kinds of stress when a child is sick or in a strange environment. Confidentiality, privacy, safety, and a feeling of security must be preserved at all times. Appropriateness is determined by the developmental age of the children being served, as well as the setting and reason for the services being received. For example, a puppet show on tooth brushing might be entertaining to elementary children in a dental clinic waiting room, but potentially frightening to a young child hospitalized for repair of a cleft palate.

Questions to ask about the content of proposed entertainment include:

- Is it appropriate to the developmental age of the children?
- Could it cause confusion or misconceptions about anything that might happen here?
- Might it engender fears and fantasies about being harmed in any way?
- Does it contain religious themes or content that might be troublesome to some families? (Religious themes and content are best avoided in non-sectarian agencies.)
- Does it carefully avoid any suggestion of violence, use of weapons, or death?
- Do performers understand that masks and certain costumes can be frightening to young children?
- Does it invite children's participation in appropriate and noncompetitive ways?
- Does it avoid the use of medical humor that might confuse children about their actual experiences here?

The staff member in charge of making decisions about the merits of entertainment will keep these guidelines in mind, as well as the scheduling requirements and space constraints of the agency. Schedules for entertainment should never be arranged without consultation with direct care staff. If entertainment is to take place on a unit or ward, sounds and sights must not be disruptive to those children and families who do not wish to participate. Entertainers wish to please, and usually will welcome specific guidelines about how to make the experience enjoyable. A verbal orientation should be reinforced with written guidelines in advance, such as those in Appendix A, page A11. For the benefit of all, the designated guide should meet and greet performers, and accompany them to run interference.

Visitors

THE SAME GUIDELINES GIVEN for entertainers apply to visitors as well. Individuals who are interested in "just visiting" the children

Special Issues: Entertainers, Visitors, Holidays, and Donated Goods

should be given information about the regular volunteer program. The potential benefits of a visit by celebrities or donors must be weighed against the possibility for disruption, invasion of privacy, and simply taking more of staff time than is warranted. Young children have little concept of celebrity and can be confused by adult reactions. Children and families must never be made to feel they are on display.

Large agencies have clear protocols for the management of professional visitors and corporate donors, based on psychosocial guidelines that take into account the needs of children and families. A designated staff person or department should handle approved visitors through the public relations or development department. It is important that consultation from professional staff qualified in child and family psychosocial issues be a part of planning and policy decisions governing visitors escorted by these departments. Stringent cautions apply to individuals who wish merely to "observe" at the agency for professional or academic reasons. Observations, unless part of a bona fide professional education program with clinical supervision, may be an invasion of privacy. Many agencies do not permit observations. An agency should have protocols worked out in advance to protect children, families, and staff.

Holidays

HOLIDAYS GENERATE ALL KINDS OF OFFERS, some welcome and some entirely unsuitable. Whenever possible, prevention is the key. Volunteer department staff at the Children's National Medical Center in Washington, D.C., developed a toy and holiday brochure to deal with the large number of inquiries about helping out at holidays. (See Appendix A, page A12.) The quality of donations improved dramatically, and donors were gratified to know that their contributions were genuinely helpful. A printed brochure not only educates the public regarding holiday celebrations and safety standards, but eliminates the need for lengthy telephone conversations.

Holidays seem to generate an outpouring of goodwill. Most of it springs from a genuine desire to be helpful. Some of it, however, seems to be based on the false assumption that agency staff has made no holiday plans for children, or that a one time attention from a stranger is just what every child longs for! It is important to reassure the public, tactfully, that the agency does indeed recognize and celebrate holidays in many special ways, and to provide specific suggestions for ways the interested public can provide support.

It is not uncommon for agencies to receive calls from individuals who wish to "take a poor unfortunate child" into their home over the holidays. Similarly, parents may call expressing a desire to bring their own children to the agency to "teach them gratitude by showing them what it is like for more unfortunate children." It is sometimes difficult to be tactful toward such misguided motivations. Generally state, "We do appreciate your interest, but it is not really appropriate. I will send you our holiday brochure, which will give you some ideas of the kinds of things that will be helpful."

Well-intentioned individuals want to be told how they can be most helpful. For example, the president of a well known philanthropic group once expressed an interest in visiting an acute care hospital on Christmas Day. Obviously, it was important to encourage his interest and goodwill. A developmental psychologist was able to say, "We are delighted that you are interested in the mission of the hospital, and will be happy to arrange a special visit for you to help you understand the needs of the children and families we serve. However, only the most acutely ill children are here on Christmas Day while the other children go home, even if they are only able to stay for a few hours. This means that the children who are here need a quiet and private family celebration more than ever. We plan for Christmas for several weeks in advance, to make sure that each family is able to celebrate in whatever way is most meaningful for them. We have a very sensitive Santa who has visited for years. Gifts are selected by staff who know the individual children. Families decide in advance whether or not they wish Santa to visit, and whether or not they wish the gifts to be presented in their name or Santa's. It is important to preserve the family privacy, as well as the child's energy level.

"So, you can see that Christmas is not the best time for a stranger to be present. We would like you to see our full services, and arrange a special time when it would be appropriate for you to see what goes on. You can understand, if your child were hospitalized here, how you might feel if we brought a stranger to observe a private family celebration." This kind of tactful education makes potential donors appreciate the quality of caring provided by an institution, and often increases their interest and commitment.

Donated Goods

IT IS ESSENTIAL IN CHILD HEALTH CARE settings to "look a gift horse in the mouth." Toys and games that might be safe in a home setting may not be so in health care agencies. For example, a board game that is suitable for an eight-year-old might not be safe to have in playroom settings where infants who might swallow small parts are present. The toy brochure in Appendix A, page A9, gives excellent guidelines, including the suggestion that wrapping paper and ribbon accompany unwrapped gifts. (This saves the time required to inspect wrapped gifts for safety.) Each agency must decide whether or not used toys will be worthwhile. Some agencies have enlisted the support of local service groups to refurbish good used toys according to safety guidelines.

An unfortunate reality is the "donor dumping syndrome" which can occur before income tax time. Donors should be informed that for income tax purposes, the agency will not attempt to make any assessment of the monetary value of donated items. The IRS requires donors to establish value with receipts.

While serving as a Director of Volunteer Services in a large pediatric hospital, I once did an April Fools' Day exhibit, for staff only, of tasteless, inappropriate, unsafe, useless, and even obscene articles donated to the hospital. Staff were invited to vote for their personal choice of "worst of show" donation, and to compose the imaginary thank you letters they would like to send for these absurd donations. It was educational, as well as cathartic.

While every donation should be acknowledged in writing, be careful not to encourage a repeat performance of the donation of useless or inappropriate items. Once protocols are established, a correspondence volunteer can handle acknowledgements. A toy brochure sent with a thank you can educate people about items that are genuinely needed. Educated donors may begin to call in advance of major holidays for a list of specific needed items, and become regular contributors because they know their contributions meet genuine needs.

Section 2

Section 2

Orientation and Training

Table of Contents

Introduction – Orientation and Training:
  Why Taking Time Saves Time 51
  ◆ What Kind of Orientation? ◆ What About Small Programs?
  ◆ You Can Succeed, One Step at a Time

2.1 – Introduction to the Agency, Job Description,
  and Environment 53
  ◆ Introducing the Job Description and Environment

2.2 – Orientation to the Volunteer Role 57
  ◆ Ways to Explore the Role

2.3 – Helping Volunteers Develop Realistic Expectations 61
  ◆ What Do Volunteers Want? ◆ Sharing Common Fears
  ◆ Taking a Realistic Look at Fears

2.4 – Policies and Procedures 67

2.5 – Special Considerations in Health Facilities 69
  ◆ Safety ◆ Infection Control ◆ Confidentiality and Privacy

2.6 – Information and Skills for Working with
  Children and Families 71
  ◆ Impact of Health Care Experiences ◆ Child Development
  ◆ Supporting Normal Development and Coping Through Play
  ◆ Books and Expressive Arts ◆ Communication Skills
  ◆ Age-Appropriate Preparation for Health Care Experiences
  ◆ Self-Reflection and Sharing Significant Observations

Introduction

Orientation and Training: Why Taking Time Saves Time

DO YOU RECOGNIZE this common refrain heard in far too many agencies?

"We don't have time to train volunteers. Isn't there some training manual we can just give them?"

Unfortunately, there is no magic training manual which will be applicable for the variety of volunteer roles in all child health settings. *In every setting, someone must take time to plan an adequate orientation and training for volunteers.* Taking this time, in fact, saves valuable time and energy. It is the only way to prevent the volunteer revolving door syndrome. The time invested in planning, training, and developing materials appropriate for the setting, will pay off in an improved program, the retention of satisfied, effective volunteers, and staff pleased with volunteer help.

What Kind of Orientation?

WHERE AGENCIES HAVE recognized the wisdom of investing time and funds in volunteer orientation and training, several kinds of programs have proven effective. These include:

- An all day group orientation, followed by pairing new volunteers with experienced volunteers.

- A one-session orientation to the agency, followed by individual self-directed learning exercises (such as those in Appendix B) that are reviewed with the direct supervisor on the job. Volunteer responsibilities are increased gradually, as competence is demonstrated.

- Group orientation and training divided into several sessions (ranging from two to four hours in length) with reading materials for homework. Discussion and reflection sessions are interspersed with practicuum sessions.

- Employment of part time staff members whose sole function is to orient, train, (and sometimes supervise) volunteers.

While the last example seems like a luxury, it can be the most cost effective. It assures thorough preparation of volunteers and higher retention and satisfaction. It eliminates overwhelming staff with added responsibilities or short-changing training for other priorities. There are many well qualified people seeking part-time employment. There is also a growing shortage of daytime volunteers in most programs, while more people seem to be available to volunteer evenings and weekends. By hiring evening and weekend trainers, many programs have been able to hold evening and weekend orientation programs and also develop new services for children and families when more volunteers are available.

What About Small Programs?

IT IS EXTREMELY DIFFICULT for the same staff member to be expected to provide direct services to children and families, as well as to develop orientation, training, and supervisory programs for volunteers. Extra time *must* be set aside for staff members to plan orientation content and sequence, develop materials, and arrange logistics. Some suggestions which might help small programs include:

- Are there qualified, active volunteers who could help with the organization of materials for orientation, and help train as well?
- Can new volunteers be paired with experienced volunteers for some orientation?
- What other staff members are qualified to help with portions of training? Including staff members from other departments often increases their support of the program.
- What can volunteers learn on their own with appropriate checklists, self-directed exercises, and follow-up with staff?
- Are there specific assignments for which volunteers can be quickly trained, and responsibilities increased after supervision?

You Can Succeed, One Step at a Time

SECTION TWO is designed as a step by step guide to orientation and training for all trainers, whatever the size of the program. It includes the basic content which must be covered for volunteers in all child health settings, as well as specific suggestions for covering each component. In reviewing succeeding chapters, you will be able to develop an outline applicable to your unique program. Your outline, and orderly sequence of instruction, should eliminate the fear that something important has not been covered.

You will not need to reinvent the wheel for training materials. Appendix B is a resource section of materials which can be photocopied for volunteers. There are articles, checklists, self-directed exercises, information sheets, and discussion questions. Adapt them to suit your setting. They will work equally well for group discussion, or as handouts for individual volunteers to complete and discuss with a supervisor. You may decide to staple several into an orientation booklet for each volunteer. Many of these materials have been generously shared by ACCH members in successful programs. Whenever you use or adapt any of these materials, always credit the source indicated.

Chapter 2.1

Introduction to the Agency, Job Description, and Environment

PERSONAL ATTENTION TO VOLUNTEERS at the point of entry should model the kind of reassurance and welcome needed by children and families in the health agency. A welcoming letter, warm personal greeting, name tags, refreshments, and attention to personal needs such as parking, restrooms, and telephones are vital. It communicates again that the agency needs, wants, and welcomes volunteers. This applies whether the orientation is for a group or an individual. Group orientations promote shared learning, a sense of camaraderie and cohesiveness, and are cost effective as well.

After a general welcome and introductions, ask volunteers what they hope to learn in orientation. Find out what they wish to know, and indicate when this information will be covered. At the beginning of each session, give an overview of what will be covered.

A beginning orientation should include: 1) an introduction to the agency and 2) an overview of the physical environment. Whether this information is presented verbally or in writing, it should be *brief*. The purpose is to provide a broad enough context for a comfortable beginning, not to overwhelm the volunteer with too much information.

VOLUNTEERS ARE USUALLY WONDERING, *"What's the purpose of this agency?" "What's this place really like?" and "What am I doing here?" Some will be wondering, "Will it be what I expected? Do I really belong here?" Do not assume volunteers have a clear understanding of the agency's overall purpose and scope of services. This agency overview should be stated in one to three paragraphs, a page at most. Many agencies have a brochure that serves this purpose.*

A brief overview description of the agency (written or verbal) should include:

- the agency name;
- operating since _(year)_ or founded in _(year)_ ;
- overall purpose or mission (don't describe every discrete service);
- types, ages, or conditions of the population served (such as "acutely ill children from birth to 19 years of age," or "pregnant youth age 12 to 18");

- region served ("this county only," or "from all over the world");
- major unique factors, such as "only outpatient clinic in county," or "first residential treatment center in this area," or "meets only 2% of estimated need for this service";
- goal of agency's service ("to make a smooth transition from hospital to home," or "to assure individualized education for children with handicapping conditions"); and
- an inclusive statement about staff ("a multi-disciplinary health care team," or "medical, nursing, and social work professionals").

Next, show, diagram, or describe verbally or with a simple handout the *overall physical plant* (not the volunteer's immediate work environment). Large agencies should provide a simplified map showing major entrances, street names, public transportation access, and locations of major service areas. In addition, describe what the volunteer will need to know to attend to their own physical needs.

A diagram or instructions should include locations for:
- Securing personal belongings;
- Restrooms;
- Eating facilities and hours;
- Public telephones;
- Public transportation;
- Taxi stands;
- Parking;
- Security;
- Agency information booth or center;
- Lost and found; and
- Library.

Provide this information as a basic one-page "where to find," but do not dwell on it. Capitalize instead on the interest and excitement of a new beginning. Warmly explain why the agency welcomes and needs volunteers, and how their roles support the mission of the agency. Volunteers need an immediate sense that their contribution will make a difference. This can be a brief verbal explanation to a group, such as: "We need volunteers to provide comfort and companionship to children in isolation... to help set up activities in the playroom... to read stories." If the volunteer is assigned to a particular service, a written description of the goals of that particular program should also be provided. This accompanies, but is separate from, the volunteer's detailed job description.

Introducing the Job Description and Environment

VERY EARLY IN ORIENTATION, the written job description should be reviewed, as it answers the volunteer's question, "What will I be doing here?" When several volunteers have the same assignment, this can be done with a group. Where there is a single volunteer assigned to a specific area, the job description can be reviewed with the direct supervisor. Each point of the job description should be covered in turn, and questions answered. Be sure to clarify at the beginning how assignments are made. With the volunteer role clearly in mind, volunteers will be better able to assess the actual work environment.

An introduction to the specific work environment should be thorough, and can be reinforced with a personal checklist. (See Appendix B, page B2.) An overview of the setting, schedule, equipment, storage, safety precautions, waste disposal, as well as demonstration and practice of basic procedures should be included. Do not expect volunteers to remember a great deal of new information. A follow-up treasure hunt, or self-directed review, such as the personal orientation checklist, can be helpful.

When the volunteer begins the assignment, introductions and an overview of who's who on the staff is important. Some agencies post photos of staff and volunteers so children and families can easily get to know them. It is also important for staff to be prepared to welcome the volunteer aboard. Every volunteer needs one supervisor, as well as clear instructions of where to turn for help if the designated supervisor is not present. The job description should spell this out.

A child life specialist encourages self-expression and free choice.

Chapter 2.2

Orientation to the Volunteer Role

THE INITIAL OBJECTIVE OF ORIENTATION is to help volunteers imagine themselves doing specific things which are needed, helpful, and rewarding. So, you present a picture of specific needs being met by specific activities. You are presenting an inspiring answer to the question "Why are we here?" Briefly describe volunteer *actions* and the results of these activities, such as "doing those nurturing things that help the child develop, such as rocking a baby or playing ping-pong with a teenager," or "making it as easy as possible for the family in a time of stress by helping a worried parent fill out forms, or reading a story to a child so parents can take a break." A photo display of volunteers engaged in specific activities is helpful.

Ways to Explore the Role

♦ Reviewing a child's experience

Presenting needs and roles by briefly describing a child's and family's "typical" experience. For example, in a hospital you might say, "If you were a child in this hospital, what might your day be like?" "You would wake up around 7:00 a.m. Breakfast is brought to your room on trays around 7:30. After breakfast, you might be bathed at the bedside, linen changed. Doctors make rounds in small groups between 8:00 and 8:30 a.m. By 9:00 a.m. you would be taken to the playroom for group activities." This is an opportunity to point out the many different adults involved in a child's care, and how this might impact any sick person. Also, it is important to point out how these routines differ from the home environment. The purpose is to give a broad scope of what a day includes for the child, to help volunteers imagine the experience from the child's perspective. "Since volunteers won't be here a whole day, it helps to know what has been happening . . . Families may visit at any time, but most working parents can only come in the evening." Describe rooming in and visiting policies.

If there are significant differences between daytime and evening activities in facilities where children stay overnight, point these out. For example, there may be more activities, interactions with staff, and distractions in the daytime. In a hospital, nurses will provide direct care, child life specialists provide play activities; physicians make rounds; various technicians, therapists, and housekeepers all may interact with children. In the evening and on weekends, the number of activities decreases and there are fewer staff.

Children may feel more lonely and vulnerable as it becomes dark outside, and they think of home. This is important contextual information for evening and weekend volunteers. Guide volunteers to imagine the experience from the child's and family's point of view.

♦ Discussing an Audiovisual

Films and videotapes are an excellent way to show what happens with children and families in a health care setting. Films you may wish to review include: *To Prepare a Child, First Do No Harm* and *A Hospital Visit with Clipper*, available from Public Relations, Children's National Medical Center, 111 Michigan Avenue, NW, Washington, DC, 20011. Films available from ACCH include: *Seasons of Caring, Family-Centered Care*, and *Pediatric Aids: A Time of Crisis*. You might suggest advance viewing guidelines, such as "Note differences in individual children's and parent's responses," "See if you can discover age-level differences," "How much choice do children have?" "Where do you see positive or supportive responses from staff?" or "Focus on one child or family and see what you can learn about their needs from their reactions."

♦ Considering Children's Reactions

Another technique is to write questions on the chalkboard and invite reflection. <u>Question</u>: "What age child do you think is most vulnerable to emotional trauma in health care? Why?" Anything that elicits discussion will help provide you with vital information about volunteers' knowledge, opinions, and openness. It also helps volunteers become acquainted with each other. For example, if you invite four answers to the question about age-level vulnerability, you stimulate a beginning discussion of the core content for pediatric volunteers: child development. You want to find out how much volunteers already know, and begin the process of shared teaching and learning. A skilled facilitator can comment appreciatively for each answer given. <u>Answer</u>: The most vulnerable age is late infancy through toddler, because children cannot comprehend separation from parents. See Appendix B, page B17.

♦ Sharing Common Experiences

An excellent way to deal with common themes is to facilitate discussion of the group's personal history with health care or hospitalization. Often, significant personal experiences which may not have been shared during interviews are forthcoming. An instructor may learn which volunteers need closer support to prevent their personal projections onto a child's experience.

Begin by asking, "Was anyone here ever hospitalized as a child?" Ask for a show of hands. It is rare to encounter a group where no one has had this experience. "We won't ask your complete medical history, but will you tell us briefly what you remember most about the experience? How old were you?" Write on the board brief notes of salient points, such as "4 y.o., tonsillectomy, ice cream, cried for mother, scary white coats." Obtain as many different responses as quickly as possible, jotting down salient points for later discussion. Thank each respondent and encourage further sharing about the impact of these experiences.

Orientation to the Volunteer Role

After sufficient sharing of a variety of experiences, ask "Have any of you ever visited someone you loved in a hospital — nursing home — health care facility?" Follow the same procedure, asking "What was it like?" In the rare event that no one in the group has had either of these experiences, ask "How do you feel when you go to the doctor? dentist?" or "Have you ever been alone in a strange place? What was it like?"

♦ Summarizing Common Fears

After listing a variety of responses about relevant feelings, you can ask the group, "Based on these memories of personal experiences we've shared, let's make a list of things children may fear in this setting." Then ask, "Based on these fears, what do they need?" Write these lists on the chalkboard. For example, the summary list of what hospitalized people fear might include such things as: the unknown, strange people, lack of information, strange equipment, pain, absence of loved ones, death, fear that staff do not know what they are doing, fear that people do not care, boredom, being all alone, having no one to talk to, and having no choices. The list of what people need will likely include such things as: clear and honest explanations, comfort, patience, and friendliness.

What Children Fear:

Age Group	Fears
Infants	Separation from parents
Toddlers	Separation, abandonment
Pre-schoolers	Abandonment, bodily harm, that they are responsible
School-age & Adolescents	Loss of control, pain, death

You can summarize with a brief outline of common age-level fears, indicating that these will be covered more fully in take-home reading, such as the article by Dr. Robinson included in Appendix B, page B16. Point out that too often a child's vulnerability is increased by health care practices that make worst fears come true. Volunteers and staff who understand these fears can provide the supports which are needed.

♦ Reflecting on Family Fears and Needs

Continue the discussion by asking the group, based on their experiences as visitors, "What do family members fear? What do they need?" Write visitors' fears and needs on the board. The list of the fears of family members might include such statements as, "Can I trust these experts?" "Will they really care?" "Do they know what they are doing?" "If I ask questions will I 'rock the boat' and make things worse?" or "If I keep quiet, will care be inadequate?"

♦ Universalizing Common Concerns and Needs

This discussion always uncovers the tip of the iceberg of some universal human fears and needs. Point this out! After sufficient discussion it is also easy to point out that human caring and intervention of some kind is usually what is wanted to meet most of the fears and needs described. What these memories usually highlight is seldom the *medical outcome* of these experiences. Rather, it is the emotions and anxieties, positive *and* negative feelings, that are vividly recalled. Those acts that convey caring, or a lack of caring, seem to be most vividly remembered. Point out that we wish to support children and families and prevent unnecessary trauma. When children and families are supported by people who understand and care, a potentially stressful experience can be turned into a positive experience where they feel they have coped and mastered a difficult time.

It is important to remind volunteers that each of them chose to come to the agency, in hopes that volunteering would be a rewarding experience. Nevertheless, all may have arrived with some second thoughts, wondering if the experience in this strange place with strange people would be what they anticipated. This is natural, even for adults who are in charge of their own activities. You might remind the group of their initial hesitations and cautious behaviors as they tested out the group and the environment when they arrived for this first session.

Imagine, however, how a child who is sick might feel about a health care experience — which they did not choose — that involves pain, uncertainty, confusion, that does not promise to be pleasurable, and that is controlled by a confusing parade of strange adults. Your group will have an immediate appreciation for the special needs of children. Parents and other family members may experience the common fears of visitors and also need special understanding and support. Volunteers can provide a warm, reassuring presence, which can make a difference at a time when children and families are most vulnerable.

♦ Relating Philosophy to Needs

Conclude the introductory session by summarizing the philosophy and goals of the program — to promote wellness and prevent trauma to children and families. "You are here to help us prevent unnecessary stress, to be the friendly presence that makes children and families feel cared for. You are not here to be medical experts, but to be yourself and provide simple human caring, which is an essential part of healing."

Your first session goal has been to inspire a sense that there are important human needs that can be met by human caring. You have presented a mission and a service opportunity that will make volunteers want to return, to be a part of this team. You have given specific examples of things volunteers do to help. By encouraging sharing of personal experiences and reactions, you have encouraged the group to form a bond of recognition of common human needs. In summarizing those needs, you have provided an experiential framework for the philosophy and goals of service.

Chapter 2.3
Helping Volunteers Develop Realistic Expectations

ANTICIPATORY GUIDANCE IS A COMMON supportive technique in both pediatrics and parenting. It is no less effective with volunteers. The primary guideline, whether with parents, children, or volunteers, is to begin where they are. To do so, you must find out what they already know and think. This is needed to correct misconceptions, fill in gaps, and give perspective in advance. There are some common hopes and fears shared by many volunteers. *Don't* begin by pointing this out! You wish, rather, to lead them in a process of *discovering* this; thus you will build ties, allay fears, and strengthen commitment.

By dealing with fantasies and fears in the beginning, when uncertainty is greatest, you put both in perspective for volunteers. This reassures volunteers that the agency appreciates their concerns and knows how to give support and encouragement. Do not mention fears until positive fantasies have been shared.

What Do Volunteers Want?

HOW DO YOU FIND OUT what volunteers are hoping for? Begin with a group discussion exercise. This exercise can help the group focus on what they anticipate the volunteer experience will be like. It encourages sharing and can help build a sense of common desires and concerns. You can invite sharing by saying, "Let's have some fun and indulge our fantasies. Let's pretend that this volunteer experience is going to turn out to be absolutely wonderful in every way. In this fantasy you will succeed beyond your wildest dreams. This will mean different things for different people, but let's share what it would mean for you personally. Someone please give us an example — What would be something that would happen in a wonderful experience here for you?"

Responses might include statements like: "I would make a child smile." "A child would be happy to see me." "I would be able to reach a child no one else was able to reach." Get as many responses as possible, and accept them all, regardless of appropriateness, including "I would meet and marry a good looking doctor!" Fantasy means anything is possible! These responses help you identify needs, desires, and values. Comment supportively, such as "Right! We all need feedback!" "We want to feel worthwhile," or "We like a challenge." You are setting a precedent for volunteers to examine and admit their feelings, a vital process for learning and growth.

Management, Selection, Training & Supervision

Section Two

Y**OU CAN SUMMARIZE THIS SHARING** by pointing out how much we all need and desire a positive result and response for our efforts. You may need to give perspective on the reality of some desires, such as "We'd be thrilled if a child hugged us and said 'I love you,' but that probably won't happen, and we shouldn't expect it. The desire for love is understandable, but that really isn't why we're here." Regarding the human need for love and relationship, point out "It is very important to recognize and admit our deepest fantasies. Only then can we learn to separate our personal needs and wishes from the needs of the child."

Regarding the normal desire for feedback, you can point out that "You will learn, through experience, to know there may be only small signs that your time makes a difference. You will learn to be satisfied, even proud, of small gains. For example, maybe you feel you 'only' rocked a baby to sleep. Ask yourself, would the baby have been alone if I had not been here? As many parents will tell you, rocking a baby to sleep is not a small accomplishment."

By universalizing and normalizing the expressed desires, you give perspective. You may also be able to identify individuals who need closer monitoring. This fantasy sharing should not be long — five to ten minutes should elicit enough responses for the laughter of recognizing the commonality of fantasies and a gentle summation by the facilitator.

Sharing Common Fears

L**IKEWISE, A SHARING OF FEARS** can be done fairly quickly, in 10 or 15 minutes. When the fantasy sharing exercise has been done in good spirit and with honesty, it is easy to say, "Now that we know we're all in this together, let's look at some other thoughts. As you anticipate volunteering, what are some of your concerns?" (with a comfortable group, "What are your worst fears?" or "What are you most afraid of?"). Do not offer suggestions — wait for responses. Fears are less easily shared than fantasies, so initial silence is normal.

Again, write the responses on the board and encourage each one. Do not make suggestions or tell the group what volunteers usually fear. Self-discovery and the courage to share are the purposes of this exercise.

Asking about fears nearly *always* elicits *some* form of the following responses from prospective pediatric hospital volunteers. Volunteers who are not involved in direct service or acute care still usually share some form of these typical concerns:

- *"What if I get too attached to a child or family?"*
- *"What if I say the wrong thing?"*
- *"What if there's a medical emergency?"*
- *"What if a child asks me if they're going to die?"*
- *"What if a child dies?"*
- *Occasionally, "What if the staff resents me?"*

The purpose of this exercise is threefold. First, to identify fears as normal and again model that self-reflection is a critical skill for successful human relations. Second, you wish to place these understandable fears into perspective. Third, you demonstrate that continuing education and supervision will address these common concerns.

Taking a Realistic Look at Fears

AFTER ELICITING ALL THE FEARS the group cares to share, you may simply choose to conclude by commenting briefly on each one and offering reassurance. Or, you may explore each fear briefly by having the group probe each fear, by asking questions such as, "What does this fear mean? Give an example of what would happen. What would you do? So, how can we prevent this from happening? What resources are available?"

It is usually sufficient to comment on the typical fears as follows:

What if I get too attached?

If you were not capable of attachment, we would not have chosen you as a volunteer. Human warmth and caring is one of the most important assets you bring to the volunteer experience. However, I am delighted you recognize that inappropriate attachment is something you must watch out for.

By asking this question, you have shown that you are aware of one of the most important cautions of volunteering with children, and that is the ability to separate your own needs from the needs of the child. This is one of your most important responsibilities, and it takes self-awareness. So, you need to be aware of this possibility in advance.

As a follow-up question, ask the group, "What would be some signs of over-attachment?" Spending too much time with one child, ignoring other children, wanting to give special favors to a child, thinking too much about the child when you're away, wanting to hurry back just to see this child, feeling that you are the one who best understands this child, wanting to maintain the relationship after the child leaves the health care setting. All of these are signs that you need to talk with a supervisor, and spend *less*, not more time, with this child. We all need attachments. However, you are here to meet the child's immediate needs, and not your own needs for attachment.

Of course, you will be more attracted to some children than others! Some children *are* more appealing! Pay attention to the kinds of children and behaviors which attract you and also those which repel you. Then consider the role your own needs play in this attraction or dislike. This helps you set your personal preferences aside and concentrate on the child's needs instead.

What if I say the wrong thing?

What might happen if you did? (Usually, the answer is "I would hurt a child's feelings, or make things worse.") Wouldn't it be wonderful if we all had a script we could follow so we'd never hurt anyone's feelings or embarrass them or ourselves! Once again, your question shows that you value the feelings and the privacy of children, so you are a sensitive caring person! As long as you have this kind of sensitivity, it is unlikely that you will blurt out something horrendous and awful! Your words may not be perfect, but your caring is likely to show through.

Frequently, because we do care so much, we want to say just the right words that will fix things, that will make everything all right, as if words could be like the mommy's kiss that makes the hurt well. However, when we're hurting we don't usually want someone to say the right *words*. We just want someone to *listen* and not be afraid to be *with* us in our hurt.

Your presence is going to communicate a lot more than your words. So, don't worry about this one! You'll get better at listening. Active listening is something we'll pursue in future training classes.

What if there's a medical emergency?

In a hospital (or health care setting), you're surrounded by medical experts. We'll teach you how to get help. Training will include what you need to know. (Obviously, in all settings the appropriate training must be provided in anticipation of emergency.)

What if a child asks me if they're going to die?

If a child actually asks you such a question, you have doubtless established a relationship of deep trust. We don't usually reveal our deepest concerns in casual relationships. The honest answer to that question is you don't know! However, you might respond by saying, "I know you have a serious condition. What is it that worries you about dying?" Try to identify the specific concern and get permission to share the concern with an appropriate staff person who can talk with the child. You can also say, "Who could we get to help us answer these questions that worry you the most? I care about you, but I don't have all the answers."

What if a child dies?

What would this mean, for you? What worries you the most? Our feelings about death and loss are an important part of training. If and when it happens, we need to support each other.

What if the staff resents me?

What might cause that? Some possible fears might be that staff may not want volunteers, may feel they are in the way, may think they don't know what they're doing. Also, staff may have their own favorite children, or want to protect children. Point out that volunteers serve only where requested by staff. Note that the working relationship should be supportive, that communication of questions and concerns works best when it becomes a habit cultivated by staff and volunteers alike. Note that staff members may at times be busy and preoccupied and volunteers can help by saying, "What can I do today that would be most helpful?"

Also mention that some volunteers fear "bothering" busy staff. In fact, staff members are likely to feel most secure about those volunteers who share their questions, concerns, and observations promptly.

Conclude by thanking group members for sharing some private thoughts, experiences, and feelings. Point out how helpful it is, through sharing with others, to learn that our thoughts and feelings are not so unusual. Point out that continuing self-awareness and acknowledgement of feelings, desires, and fears help place them in perspective. Point out that the agency will provide training and supervision, and will rely on the volunteer to take responsibility for his/her personal growth and skill development through the shared discussion of experiences. For homework, assign specific readings to review the psychological impact of hospitalization.

Chapter 2.4

Policies and Procedures

WRITTEN POLICIES AND PROCEDURES provide a structure and order for volunteer programs. It is important that each volunteer have a copy of the agency's policy governing volunteer services and general procedures as well. These should be reviewed early in orientation.

Policies and procedures are essential but uninteresting. Therefore it is advisable first to capture the volunteer's interest in the agency's mission and the volunteer role. Once this has meaning to the volunteer, policies and procedures will have more relevance. Written policies and procedures enable review, and eliminate the expectation that volunteers will remember a lot of new information. However, actions that will result in dismissal should be made clear from the beginning.

Policies need not be complex to be comprehensive. Avoid formal language and technical jargon. Appendix A, page A8, includes a sample of concise, comprehensive policies and procedures for volunteers.

Volunteer procedures encompass those that are expected of all volunteers, regardless of job description or assignment. This includes the how-tos of such things as signing in and out, identification, absences, scheduling, change of assignments, appropriate conduct, and emergencies. Procedures that apply only to specific volunteer jobs should be covered in the orientation to the individual work environment.

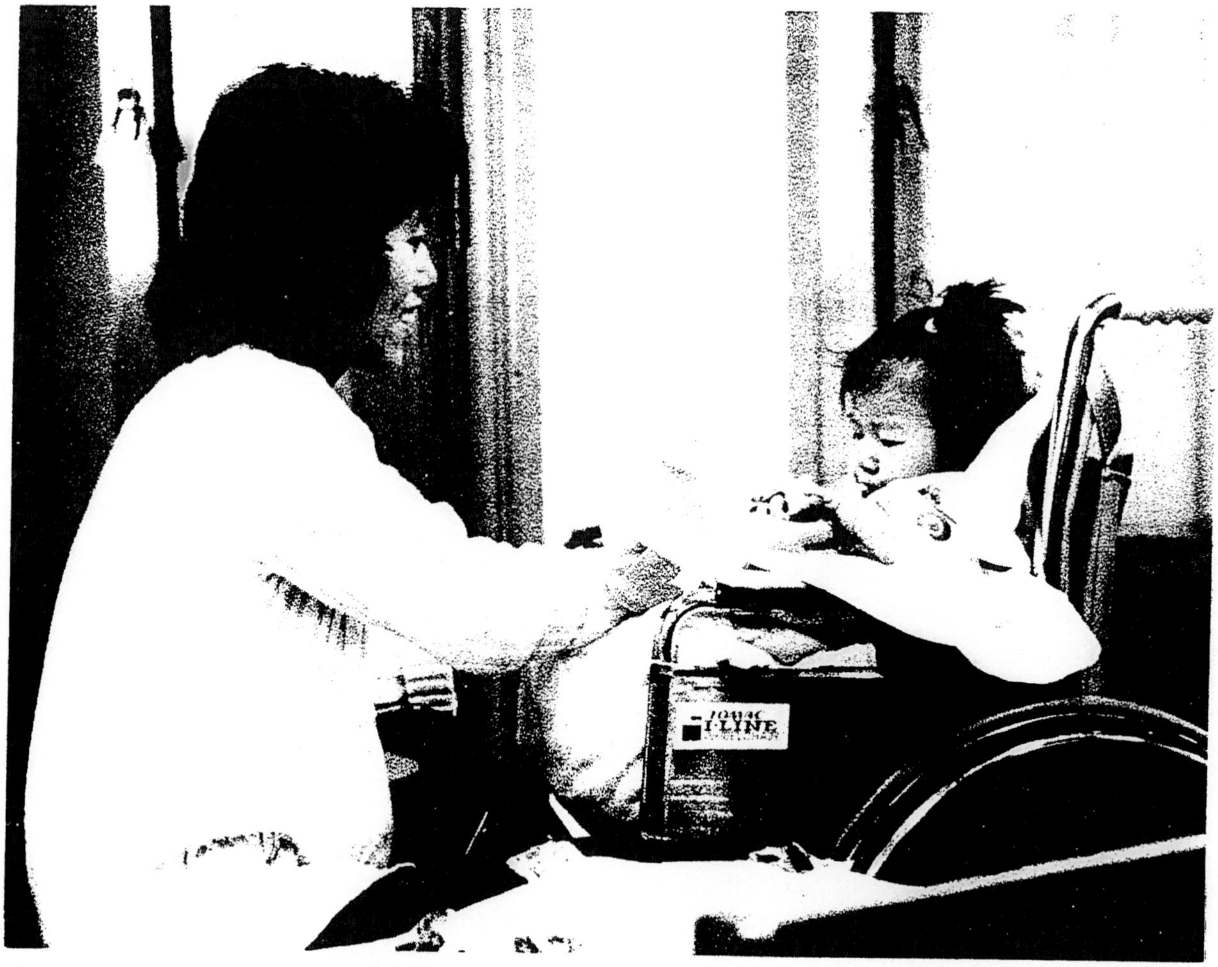
I-LINE

Chapter 2.5: Special Considerations in Health Facilities

Safety, confidentiality, privacy, and infection control are four topics which must be covered explicitly with all health care volunteers.

Safety

KEEPING THE ENVIRONMENT SAFE at all times requires eternal vigilance. Agencies *can be held liable for any accidents resulting from failure to teach safety to volunteers*. While it is not possible to write guidelines that are comprehensive enough for all types of pediatric facilities, the checklist in Appendix B, page B3, can serve as a guide and reminder of important points that must be taught to volunteers. Extra lines allow you to add items to the checklist. Be sure to cross out items that do not apply to volunteers in your setting. The safety checklist can be covered in sections and reviewed frequently. You must supplement this list with information specific to your setting. *Do not rely on printed materials alone*. Remember to demonstrate, discuss, and observe volunteers practicing important common procedures. These can be modeled by an individual, or done with audiovisuals, provided they are discussed. The Johns Hopkins Child Life Department uses a safety video and has volunteers look for and discuss unsafe practices. Volunteers should practice, with supervision, all safety procedures, such as the correct way to raise and lower crib side rails, hold a baby, or put on and dispose of isolation garments.

Infection Control

INFECTION CONTROL BEGINS with enforcing the local health policies governing paid and volunteer staff in pediatric agencies. Teaching and observing simple handwashing is the single most effective means of infection control. Specific isolation procedures will vary according to the scope of services offered by an agency. Appendix B materials include an overview of the basic principles for all settings, as well as a simple overview of isolation categories, including HIV infection and universal precautions. Protocols change. Keeping infection control procedures current should be the designated responsibility of a qualified individual in every health care agency. *It is essential that appropriate instruction for volunteers be included whenever new protocols are introduced.*

Section Two

Confidentiality and Privacy

VOLUNTEERS DO NOT AUTOMATICALLY know all that confidentiality and privacy encompass. Some agencies have volunteers sign a contract agreeing to keep all information confidential. Appendix B, page B8, includes a sample contract, as well as an exercise and handout describing confidentiality and privacy, pages B9-11. However, *it is essential that this information be discussed in detail with volunteers.*

Chapter 2.6: Information and Skills for Working with Children and Families

IN ORDER TO WORK COMPETENTLY and sensitively with children and families in health care settings, volunteers need to know:

- The impact of illness, hospitalization, and health care experiences on children and families;
- Child development;
- How to support normal development and coping through play;
- Communication skills;
- The importance of age-appropriate preparation for health care experiences;
- Self reflection and sharing significant observations; and
- When and how to refer children and families for additional support by staff.

The Impact of Health Care Experiences

THE IMPACT OF ILLNESS AND HOSPITALIZATION has been beautifully described in Appendix B, page B16, in an article by Mary Robinson, a former Director of Child Life. This paper, first presented at an ACCH affiliate meeting, has educated hundreds of volunteers in understanding a hospital experience from the child's point of view. The psychological impact is relevant whether or not volunteers serve in hospitals. This article may be photocopied and used for required reading, followed by discussion. Consider giving some guiding questions to be answered along with each reading you use.

One way to understand the impact of health experiences is to take a careful look at the sequence of events as the child and family might experience them in your setting. The agency routine is the norm for staff; it is seldom the norm for a child and family. Stress and anxiety exist in ambulatory as well as in overnight or residential settings. Some guiding questions could include:

- What happens when the child and family first arrive?
- How are they introduced to the agency?

- What could be done to make their arrival more comfortable?
- What happens when children and families must wait? What attention or services could reduce stress at these times?
- How do children and families find their way around a strange place? How can staff and volunteers help?
- What about brothers, sisters, and other family members?
- What special stresses surround emergency visits? What extra help is needed?
- How are children and families prepared to leave?

These questions could be used as a reflective handout for volunteers, or a guide for a group discussion. The child's age and developmental stage, and the family's unique characteristics and preferences are important variables and are necessary to consider in understanding each child and family's unique experience.

Family-centered care is now acknowledged as the standard for best care in child health. Volunteers are frequently in an ideal position to give support to the family. Volunteers can be sensitized to ask continually, "What else can we do to support and strengthen the family?" Two handouts for volunteers, Family-Centered Care, and Guidelines for Supporting Families, can be found in Appendix B, pages B29-B32. The film, *Family-Centered Care,* and the book, *Family-Centered Care for Children with Special Health Care Needs,* provide further information. Both are available from ACCH. Some pediatric hospitals are establishing family resource libraries, using volunteers to help with materials for children and adults. The publication *Guidelines for Establishing a Family Resource Library* is available from ACCH.

Child Development

VOLUNTEERS' FORMAL KNOWLEDGE of child development can range from extensive to non-existent. There are many excellent written materials on child development, and volunteers will vary in their interest and ability to pursue this information. *It is important for volunteers to have a general understanding of the expected sequence of normal development and children's individuality, and also to be aware of their own individual opinions about development.* Some articles on child development, written for volunteers, are included in Appendix B, pages B33-43.

Do not make the mistake of assuming volunteers will not read articles! Many careers have been launched by nurturing a volunteer's curiosity about human development. It is important to keep child development reference materials updated for interested volunteers. Encourage volunteers with this particular interest to update a bibliography and share resources they have found that will help other volunteers. A balance of some classic text plus contemporary magazine articles is helpful.

Information and Skills for Working with Children and Families

Supporting Normal Development and Coping Through Play

HOW CAN VOLUNTEERS BEST BE PREPARED for that most vital role, facilitating play? Play is essential for learning, growth, and development of all children. Play is the child's means for exploring the world and discovering possibilities. During the stress of a health care experience, a child needs play more than ever. Play not only provides opportunities for enhancing normal development, but can help the child and family master a difficult experience. The nature and scope of an agency's play program will vary according to the ages of children served, the acuity of care, the space, and the available staff, including volunteers. A comprehensive play program staffed by child development professionals, frequently called a child life program, is the recognized standard for quality pediatric programs.

In large settings, it may be possible to group children according to age for play activities. Many settings, however, must provide a wide range of activities for several age levels simultaneously. While it is not possible to design a manual that would serve the play training needs for all settings, handouts on play and some general articles written for volunteers and self-directed exercises are included in Appendix B, pages B44-63, to augment your program. These materials can be photocopied directly and given to volunteers. Because play is creative and dynamic, new learnings are always possible. Good programs will continually update reference materials on play and child development for volunteers.

♦ Play: Orientation and Training Components for Volunteers

Whatever the setting, volunteers need to be familiar with:

- the kinds of activities and equipment which are appropriate at different age levels;
- the wide range of individuality and personal preferences expressed through play;
- some of the goals of play in a health care setting;
- how to promote play without being overly controlling;
- how to anticipate and prevent conflicts in the play areas; and
- the adult's role in creating a safe and inviting environment, offering appropriate choices, and encouraging without directing.

In addition to the skills required to facilitate play, volunteers and others need practical information about schedules and equipment. Good programs will have written information for the following:

- daily schedule for play and recreational activities including group play, individual play, and play for children in isolation;
- protocol for playroom and equipment use;
- suggestions for age-appropriate materials and activities for individuals and groups;

- posted checklist for opening and setting up play areas; and
- a posted checklist for clean-up, equipment storage, and closing play areas. Posting this information promotes the play program and invites others to help maintain order.

Each agency should provide written procedures regarding the following information:

- play equipment (indoor and outdoor if available);
- toy safety;
- equipment storage, care, and availability;
- hygiene procedures such as disinfecting toys;
- protocol for toys used in isolation;
- location acceptable for group activities; and
- activity suggestions for groups and individuals.

The self-directed exercise in Appendix B, page B5, will reinforce the volunteer's understanding of this information.

After training is completed, it is necessary to observe each volunteer's performance before deciding when they may work appropriately with children without supervision. Competent volunteers can greatly extend the play program by working one-on-one with assigned children, or supervising small groups and thus relieving professional staff for other activities.

Volunteers may be encouraged to bring in their own play materials, provided these materials meet safety standards. In planning activities, remind volunteers that even those activities a child rejects serve a purpose. A child has been able to exercise freedom of choice in a setting that must impose many treatments and limits on the child. Some programs find it helpful to prepare book carts, art carts, or tote bags of materials for volunteers to check out from a central location and take to the play site. You can encourage donations of materials with a list of the most desirable materials and books. The toy brochure, Appendix A, page A12, can serve as a guideline.

Books and Expressive Arts

THE HEALING AND DEVELOPMENTAL POTENTIAL of books and expressive art activities cannot be overestimated. Providing a variety of materials and activities, freedom of choice, plenty of time for exploration, and encouraging process and individual expression rather than prescribed products are important guidelines expanded upon in the handout in Appendix B, page B67. Family members will welcome activities that encourage their participation. In addition, separately scheduled diversionary activities for parents are greatly appreciated in settings where children remain for long periods.

Information and Skills for Working with Children and Families

An excellent reference is *Very Special Arts for Children in Hospitals* by J. Rollins (in press), available from Very Special Arts, Washington, D.C. A local children's librarian can be consulted to suggest appropriate books for children and families.

Communication Skills

A WARM AND SUPPORTIVE PRESENCE communicates more than words. Nevertheless, words are important. Communication needs will vary according to the scope of the volunteer's role. Some materials written for volunteers are included in Appendix B, pages B68-71. Communications skills should be anticipated and practiced using specific examples from the agency setting.

This can be in the form of a handout, group discussion of problem situations, or role plays.

For example, volunteers need to know how to introduce themselves graciously to children and families, how to take their leave, how to offer help, give directions, prepare children in advance for changes in activities, communicate acceptance and respect, listen empathetically and nonjudgmentally, prevent and control unruly behaviors, enable children and parents to express feelings freely, and when and how to seek help.

Age-Appropriate Preparation for Health Care Experiences

PREPARATION FOR HEALTH CARE EXPERIENCES is a vital part of preventing unnecessary trauma. Preparation is primarily the responsibility of staff qualified to do developmentally appropriate interventions with children. However, volunteers need to know what kind of preparation the agency offers children and families, who does the preparation and the rationale behind preparation. Medical play is a component of preparation. Because children may spontaneously engage volunteers in medical play, volunteers need to understand basic principles, as well as the importance of sharing observations with staff. Child Life Director Sally Francis' article on Medical Play, Appendix B, page B72, gives an excellent overview. In using this article, it is essential to clarify for volunteers the limitations of their role in medical play.

Self-Reflection and Sharing Significant Observations

IN WORKING WITH CHILDREN, it is important to be a careful observer of the child and of one's own reactions as well. Self-reflection is a critical human-relations skill. When analyzing and reflecting on volunteer experiences becomes a habit, it is possible to evaluate skillfully, seek help when needed, make changes, and grow. Children and families will be helped in proportion to a volunteer's ability to make sensitive observations and follow through appropriately. This habit can best be cultivated by staff who routinely ask volunteers "How did it go today?" This models that reflection, feedback, and sharing are valued.

When working with children and families, it is important for volunteers to be flexible and adaptable to changing needs by paying attention to cues from the child. The articles on play, child development, and communication skills in Appendix B give many guidelines. Volunteers may not find it easy to attend simultaneously to the child and to their own personal reactions. Volunteers can be encouraged to make a habit of reflecting on the volunteer experience at the conclusion of each work period. This allows attention to feelings and thoughts that may not have reached conscious awareness during the actual experience. Just as children have different preferred styles, so do adults. Some volunteers may find it helpful to reflect quietly alone, to write in a journal (as long as no names or confidential information is used), or to discuss any questions with a fellow volunteer or supervisor.

Appendix B, page B75 and B77, includes an exercise that encourages reflection, a handout on sharing important observations with staff, and a self-evaluation guide for volunteers.

Section 3

Section 3

The Art of Supervision

Table of Contents

Introduction	79
3.1 – What Is Supervision?	81
3.2 – Why Supervise?	83
3.3 – Barriers to Supervision	85
3.4 – Communicating Expectations	89
◆ Supervisor's Preferences ◆ Other Considerations	
3.5 – Assessment	93
3.6 – Understanding Your Preferences	95
3.7 – The Individual Supervisory Plan	99
Guidelines for Planning Individual Supervision	
3.8 – Promoting Volunteers	103
3.9 – Improving Performance: Coaching vs. Criticism	105
3.10 – Practicing Supervision: Eight Opportunities	107
◆ Group Instructions for Supervisory Opportunities ◆ Role-Play Observers' Worksheet	
3.11 – Conclusion: Supervisory Skills Review and Action Plan	129
◆ What Good Supervisors Do ◆ Supervisory Development Action Plan	

Introduction

The Art of Supervision

SINCE THE DIRECT SUPERVISOR of each volunteer has the greatest impact on the volunteer's performance and commitment, good supervision is essential for success. However, education in how to supervise others is not always included in the curriculum of health professionals. Many professionals face the classic supervisor's dilemma of being expected to learn how to supervise volunteers (and others) on the job. When programs are understaffed, people who need volunteers have little time to develop their skills, plan ahead, or reflect on direct supervisory opportunities. A cycle of reactive management — rather than anticipation, prevention, and improvement of skills — becomes the norm. The problem is further compounded when people who feel uncomfortable in the role of supervisor avoid supervisory responsibilities.

Wise administrators recognize that supervision is a learned art. It is necessary to give staff time and resources to improve supervisory skills. Since volunteers may be the best help available in many programs, the time spent improving supervisory skills may be one of the most valuable activities staff can undertake. The rewards include the satisfactions of individual growth, encouraging best performance in others, and expanding services to children and families.

This section is a guided curriculum for direct supervisors of volunteers. The principles will be equally useful for staff members who wish to improve their skills supervising other employees. A commentary on the principles of supervision is interspersed with skill-building exercises. The material should be covered in sequence, as the required reflection, application of information, and problem-solving skills increase in complexity.

The curriculum is designed for individual or group use. Individual practitioners will find it helpful to share their reflections with a colleague or supervisor. Groups of 5 to 20 supervisors may cover the information in a few sessions. It is also possible to complete the entire curriculum in a half-day inservice. Group leaders should become thoroughly familiar with the materials in advance, and photocopy the exercises for each individual member.

The goals of this section are:

- to clarify the purpose and effects of supervision;
- to analyze barriers to supervision;
- to practice some supervisory skills; and
- to develop a personal action plan.

Chapter 3.1

What Is Supervision?

Exercise

What Do Supervisors Do?

You have already experienced many kinds of supervisors in your lifetime. Reflect on the people who have supervised you.

1. Who is the best supervisor you have ever had? Think about this individual. What, exactly, did this person do? Jot down several specific behaviors.

   How did these behaviors affect your performance?

2. Recall the worst supervisor you ever had. Jot down exactly what this individual did, or did not do.

   How did these behaviors affect your performance?

3. Based on the above reflections, make a list of the things good supervisors do:

4. What do individuals need from a supervisor?

Management, Selection, Training & Supervision

Section Three

Commentary

YOU WILL READILY SEE, based on your own experience, that good supervisors are those who make expectations clear, encourage good performance, and provide continuing, constructive feedback and recognition. The result is that the individual supervised feels welcomed, useful, and appreciated; gains confidence and competence; becomes invested in the program; and can make a valuable contribution. The actions and effects of poor supervision are quite the opposite, leaving everyone dissatisfied. Volunteers, when asked these same questions, echo this consensus.

Volunteers report that a "good" supervisor:

- "made me feel my role was useful."
- "treated me like a capable person who performed a valuable task."
- "made me feel welcomed, that I wasn't wasting time or in the way."
- "let me do anything I felt comfortable doing."
- "opened my eyes about dealing with children who are seriously ill, and how families cope with it."
- "guided me well, allowed me to seek my own level."

In contrast, a "poor" supervisor:

- "didn't give specific examples of what to do — so I felt awkward just wandering in."
- "was too busy, so I didn't know what to do."
- "couldn't be specific as to where help was needed."
- "was unable to welcome me into her world."

It is clear which experiences would induce a volunteer to return. And this leads us to consider why supervision is vital to a good program.

Chapter 3.2: Why Supervise?

Exercise

What is the purpose of supervision?
Jot down your answers to this question.

Commentary

THERE ARE THREE BASIC PURPOSES of supervision:

1. to see that the job is done according to defined program objectives and performance standards;
2. to monitor performance and make needed changes; and,
3. to encourage the best possible performance from each individual.

Source: Arlene Kiely, Training Consultant, ACCH, Bethesda, MD

Overall, the desired outcome is to promote competent, independent performance, freeing the supervisor to further expand and improve the program.

The process of supervision is a continuing cycle of:
- defining needs;
- communicating expectations;
- monitoring performance; and
- giving and receiving feedback.

When the process results in a redefinition of needs, the cycle begins anew. This is the ongoing process of a good working relationship.

A group of child life specialists, experienced in supervising volunteers, were asked, "Where do supervisors of volunteers fail?" Their answers focused on planning, expectations, and continuity. Failure to take the time to plan program objectives and define the volunteer's role, having unrealistic expectations of volunteers, and failure to assess and communicate daily were the mistakes most commonly cited. These failures correspond precisely to the cycle of skills involved in good supervision: defining, communicating, and monitoring.

If the supervisory process is so simple, why do so many avoid doing it? In beginning an analysis of what is needed for a personal action plan, this is an important question to ask. The supervisory avoidance syndrome is a common phenomenon.

Chapter 3.3: Barriers to Supervision

Exercise

What Stands in the Way?

Instructions: Reflect on your own responsibilities as a supervisor. Be as specific and complete as possible, and list those things which stand in the way of your best performance.

1. Things which hinder my best performance as a supervisor include:

2. Which of the above are personal (internal) hindrances? Which are programmatic (external) hindrances? Separate the two categories.

   Personal   *Programmatic*

3. Which of these hindrances are within my power to change or control?

4. What will be required to change each of the above?

Source: Arlene Kiely, Training Consultant, ACCH, Bethesda, MD

Section Three

Commentary

THE PREVIOUS EXERCISE SHOULD HELP clarify the need to identify the source of a barrier in order to make a realistic action plan. There are external realities in every work setting. Many will require ongoing negotiation with others to meet changing program needs. External factors can usually best be addressed in terms of overall program objectives. You may need to consult with others and work out compromises, based on competing needs or schedules. You may need to take the time to plan work more carefully. You may decide to change the program.

(If, however, you are in a setting where your input is not invited regarding the kind of volunteer help desired, or if you are expected to receive volunteers without advance notice, you may find it helpful to read Chapter 1.1, "Always Include Staff," and share it with your supervisor!)

Once identified, many external barriers to supervision seem easier to correct than one's internal resistance. Internal, personal avoidance behaviors may be so habitual that they are unconscious. Yet the reasons for avoidance may sometimes provide the clues for what is needed to overcome the supervisory avoidance syndrome.

For example, many professionals admit that they deliberately avoid taking an active supervisory role because they: fear being disliked, fear hurting another person's feelings, feel awkward being in a position superior to older individuals (who may have many years of childrearing experience), or don't know how to give needed correction without sounding bossy or negative. These fears indicate recognition that good supervision will produce quite opposite results. So, how do you make this happen? Good supervision is coaching, not criticizing. People who fear causing the negative reactions are already in touch with appropriate values for being an effective supervisor.

PROFESSIONALS TRAINED IN CHILD DEVELOPMENT already have the knowledge base and values required for encouraging good performance from volunteers. They understand the importance of providing a welcoming environment, assessing and respecting individual coping and learning styles, and clarifying expectations and parameters for children. Identical guidelines apply to working with volunteers. Your approach as a supervisor should model the same kind of approach that encourages a child's self-esteem. This is not to imply that volunteers should be treated like children, but that the same principles of respect and preparation apply to volunteers in a new environment.

One of the biggest pitfalls is assuming that there are some things volunteers should not have to be told or shown. Do volunteers working with you know exactly what is expected of them? If not, why not? It is essential first to have a precise, written description of the volunteer's role. What kind of help is needed? What behaviors and functions define the volunteer's job? Is it crystal clear to volunteers what duties are always to be done? Which activities may

Barriers to Supervision

be undertaken at the volunteer's discretion? What actions are absolutely forbidden?

No one should be expected to do a job that has not been first clearly defined. If you do not yet have written job descriptions for volunteers, it is essential to stop now to review Chapter 1.4 and complete the exercise in Appendix A, page A2.

Clarifying the volunteer's role and writing a job description are essential first steps in the supervision process. Orienting volunteers to the overall agency — programs, goals, and work environment — as covered in Section II, are the next steps. After the initial orientation, good supervisors will continue to communicate expectations in the work setting, monitor individual performance, give and get feedback, and make changes as needed. What, then, are the skills required for effective communication, assessment, and feedback?

Section Three

Volunteers in Child Health:

Chapter 3.4

Communicating Expectations

IT IS UNREALISTIC TO EXPECT that volunteers will automatically understand the reasons for desired and expected behaviors. **All performance standards should be based on program objectives.** When there is a clear and beneficial reason for an expected behavior, this becomes the rationale for instruction.

Teaching, demonstrating, modelling, and giving constructive feedback is then done not from a position of criticism, but as encouragement toward a program goal. For example:

- *We want to preserve privacy, so we always knock before entering a room.*
- *It is important to allow time to clean up properly so the materials will be in order for the next play session.*
- *We find it works best to give the children advance warning that "Pretty soon it will be clean-up time." They are less likely to feel interrupted or frustrated and are more likely to cooperate.*
- *We must keep the small beads locked up to prevent the possibility of young children swallowing them.*

It is a helpful exercise for supervisors to take time to *relate each point of the volunteer's written job description to a specific program goal*. This will prepare you to communicate expectations in a manner that makes sense and develops the volunteer's confidence in the program.

Exercise

How to Relate Expected Behaviors to Program Goals

Instructions:

1. Use a copy of a volunteer job description written for your situation.
2. Number each item listed in the job description.
3. Opposite *each item* of the description, write down the *reason* for it.

Management, Selection, Training & Supervision

Section Three

Supervisor's Preferences

IT IS NATURAL FOR INDIVIDUAL SUPERVISORS to have preferred ways of doing things. People work best when allowed to develop a personal style and structure. One need not be apologetic about this. A supervisor should explain personal preferences to volunteers simply and directly: "I prefer to keep these in the blue box because it is easier to find when I need it." Or, "If you will always be sure to do this, it will be such a help to me." Decide what is important for your own comfort and be sure these things also are explained in advance.

Volunteers want to be helpful. Clear explanations tell them how they can best help. A less than desirable performance by a volunteer is frequently due to an inadequate explanation, particularly because the volunteer does not know why it is important to do things a certain way. Prevention is always easier than correction.

Exercise

Clarifying Personal Preferences

Instructions: Beyond the items in a volunteer's written job description, what procedures and tasks are important for the way you manage your program? On a separate sheet of paper:

1. List those things you wish volunteers to know.
2. Write a simple explanatory phrase for each one.
3. Which of these, if any, might need to be reinforced with written explanations or a posted checklist?

Other Considerations

VOLUNTEERS ALSO NEED A CLEAR understanding of the normal sequence of daily events, a schedule of what to do and when to do it. What volunteers can expect of the program and what volunteers can expect of staff must also be communicated. For example:

- What is the volunteer expected to do first on arrival? — Find the supervisor? Read a posted schedule? Set up equipment? Wait until someone tells them what to do?
- Where does a volunteer turn when the primary supervisor is not present?
- What can a volunteer do when there is "nothing to do?"

Anticipatory guidance for these situations is as important as preparing volunteers for unusual emergencies. Even after the best initial communication of expectations, it will be necessary to assess performance, give and get feedback, and, at times, correct poor performance. Assessment is a critical supervisory skill.

Chapter 3.5 — Assessment

EVERYONE WISHES FOR THOSE well-trained, experienced volunteers who immediately demonstrate such a high level of competence that little further supervision is needed. Happily, careful selection and orientation can produce many such individuals. However, it is unrealistic to expect that all volunteers will function in this manner. How does a supervisor assess a volunteer's capabilities, strengths, and weaknesses, and determine which volunteers need more supervision?

Exercise

Initial Assessment of Volunteer Performance

What is it that you need to know about each volunteer assigned to you, before you can comfortably assign them to work independently? (In short, what do you need to assess?) Jot down at *least six things*.

Management, Selection, Training & Supervision

Section Three

Commentary

IN GENERAL, A SUPERVISOR NEEDS to be satisfied about each volunteer's:

- understanding of what is expected;
- level of comfort with the assignment;
- readiness for a new assignment;
- ability to interact appropriately with children and families;
- willingness and ability to follow instructions and procedures;
- ability to use good judgment;
- motivation; and,
- dependability and commitment.

Assessment requires that the supervisor observe actual performance and give and get feedback. A good selection process will have addressed motivation, dependability, and commitment; however, these must be evaluated continually by the supervisor.

The volunteer's first assignment should set the tone for a positive working relationship. The volunteer needs to feel welcomed and useful from the beginning. The supervisor needs to observe and assess the volunteer's capabilities during the first assignment. A first assignment should be simple and specific, done in the presence of the supervisor as a part of a routine day. Helping with daily routines, such as set-up and clean-up, should be expected as a part of the routine, and not be optional. However, if there is a choice about direct caregiving activities, it is wise to assess the volunteer's level of comfort with a new activity. Some volunteers adapt quickly, while others need more initial support.

FOR EXAMPLE, YOU MAY ASK, "How would you like to rock this baby, and hold him so he can watch the activities in the playroom?" or, "Would you rather help the children mix clay or feed this child who is in isolation?" Ideally, you want to prepare volunteers to be flexible to meet changing needs. Beginning with an assignment that is comfortable allows the volunteer to feel useful immediately. Where there are many possibilities for assignment, knowing that a volunteer prefers infants or feels challenged by a one-on-one assignment enables the supervisor to capitalize on individual preferences. Satisfaction encourages commitment.

Volunteers can develop new skills with appropriate encouragement and instruction. "I know you're more comfortable with infants, but there is a teenager who really needs some attention. If I could introduce you, he would probably enjoy playing a game with you." Many volunteers have thus discovered hidden talents, or been encouraged to develop new skills because the supervisor presents a need and expresses confidence in the volunteer's ability to meet the need.

Chapter 3.6

Understanding Your Preferences

WHAT HAPPENS WHEN THERE ARE so many different kinds of volunteers and supervisors? To help move from speculation to reality, let's analyze some real supervisory possibilities. **Note:** The exercises in this chapter are most instructive when done by several individuals in a group who then can share answers. Parts I, II, and III are for individual or group use. Part IV is for group use only.

Exercise

Part I: Personal Preferences

Instructions: In this exercise, assume that your work setting serves children of all ages. Read the following descriptions of new volunteers who might be assigned to you. Next, rank each volunteer in order of your *personal preference* for having them assist you (1 for most preferred, 7 for least preferred). There are no right or wrong answers.

_____ a. Alice is a talented artist who travels with her own inexhaustible "bag of tricks" of things to make and do. She likes to work at a table with a group and does not enjoy working in isolation or with individual children for long periods.

_____ b. Betty is a very quiet young woman. She seems quite shy; she would rather sit in a private room and rock a baby than interact with children in the playroom.

_____ c. Charlotte is the mother of three grown children. She completed an M.A. in child development before she "retired into marriage and motherhood." She has always wanted to be a nursery school director.

_____ d. Dan is a college honors student majoring in psychology. When he was 12, his younger brother died of leukemia. Dan's primary interest is in working with dying children.

_____ e. Elsie is a calm but outgoing woman who relates very well to adults. She has engaged several individual parents in lengthy conversations and seems to be a good listener. She seems generally more attentive to adults than to children.

_____ f. Fran has 6 grown children and 12 grandchildren. She is proud of and devoted to her close family. She has definite ideas about child rearing and expresses her ideas freely.

_____ g. Gary is a retired man who has no experience with children. He is quiet, needs a lot of direction, and sometimes seems to be at a loss to know where to begin.

Source: Arlene Kiely, Training Consultant, ACCH, Bethesda, MD
Adapted from: Roxane Kaufmann, Georgetown Child Development Center, Washington, D.C.

Exercise

Part II: Understanding Preferences

Next, go back and jot down the reasons for your rankings of the volunteers just described.

a.   e.

b.   f.

c.   g.

d.

Now, analyze the reasons for each of your rankings. Consider the individuals you most and least preferred.

◆ What is the basis of your choice? Was your choice based on a personal reason? (For example, you feel you can easily manage someone who just wants to rock babies.)

◆ Was your choice based on a programmatic consideration? (Such as, you have many waiting parents and need someone who relates well to them.) Or was your choice based on a mixture? (Such as, you aren't very artsy crafty and need a volunteer who is.) Or, were your choices based on a caution or warning signal? (Such as, why does a person prefer to work with dying children? Will he be effective, or has he unfinished grief work?)

Commentary

AS A SUPERVISOR, you make decisions and act upon them daily. It is important to understand the *basis* for the supervisory decisions you make. Some will be driven by the special needs of the *program*. Others will be driven by the structure or *system* in which you work. Others will be personal, perhaps even peculiar, to your *individuality*. Others will be *cautionary*, meaning that you need more observation and information before you are comfortable making a judgment and assignment. Decisions may also be based on a combination of these factors.

When you are clear about the basis for your reaction, you will be able to make decisions more quickly, and also to evaluate conflicting forces and decide what decision is most appropriate to the needs in your setting.

Understanding Your Preferences

Exercise

Part III: Analyzing Choices

Return to the previous exercise and evaluate the basis of the rankings you made. Indicate with a P, S, I, C (or combination) the basis for your choices.

P = Program   S = System   I = Individuality   C = Caution

Exercise

Part IV: Group Discussion Instructions

If the previous exercises have been done in a group:

Have each member indicate which of the seven volunteers they most preferred to work with and give the reasons why.

Next, have each person indicate the least preferred volunteer and give reasons. Did anyone most prefer someone else's least preferred individual? Why? What does this teach about preferences and choices?

Commentary

THE VOLUNTEER SERVICE of each of the seven individuals described can be a potential success or disaster. What influences whether a volunteer becomes competent and dependable, or ineffective, or decides to drop out next week? The sensitivity and effectiveness of the supervisor is usually the key.

It is important for supervisors to recognize three things:

1. Monitoring and analyzing your own reactions is a critical skill.
2. Personal preferences influence judgment.
3. Your judgments form the basis for your supervisory plan.

Section Three

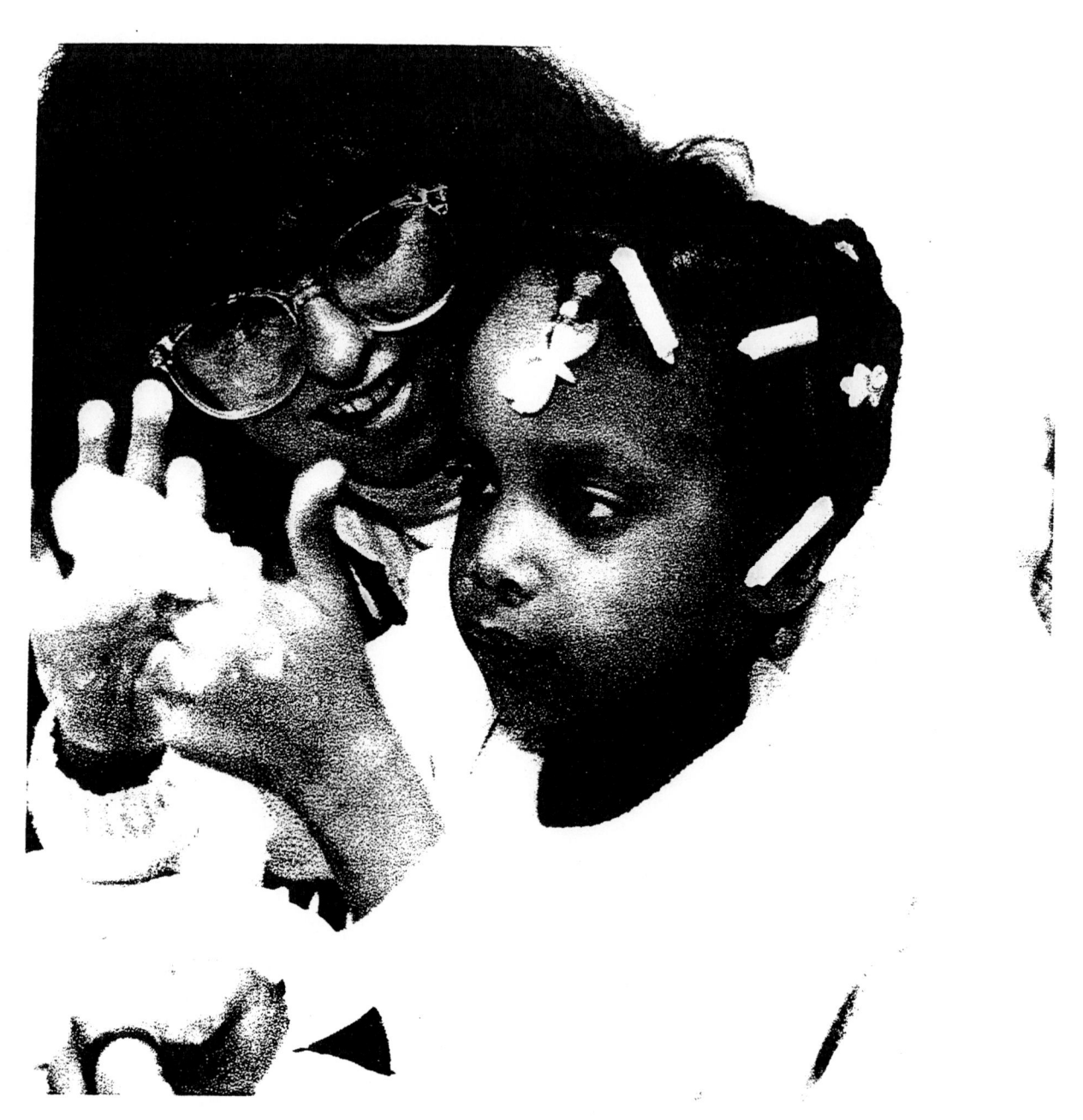

A good supervisor models supportive approaches.

Chapter 3.7

The Individual Supervisory Plan

TYPICALLY, IT SHOULD NOT BE NECESSARY to write down a supervisory plan for each volunteer you supervise. What *is* important is that a supervisor have a clear plan in mind.

Your supervisory plan for an individual volunteer is simply:

- What you feel you need to assess;
- What you will need to teach; and
- What behaviors will indicate to you that the individual needs more or less supervision. (Of course, in a structured, formal internship program where there are specific educational and behavioral objectives, a written supervisory plan may be advisable.)

Guidelines for Planning Individual Supervision

ANOTHER WAY TO ORGANIZE supervisory plans for individual volunteers is to focus on information needed and behaviors desired. Guiding questions include:

1. What information do I need to know about this individual?
2. What behaviors do I need to assess in this individual?
3. What information do I need to give this individual in:

    - Orientation
    - Making an assignment

4. What information (feedback) do I need from this individual?
5. What are my goals for this individual?

    - Ideal
    - Satisfactory

6. What behaviors will demonstrate that these goals have been accomplished?

Section Three

Exercise

Planning Supervision for an Individual Volunteer

Instructions: Imagine that the individual you *least* preferred (from the previous exercise) is assigned to volunteer with you.

1. What do you need to assess about this particular individual?

2. What might you need to teach?

3. How will you go about this? What would be a good first assignment?

4. What behaviors will demonstrate to you that the volunteer can work alone?

Source: Arlene Kiely, Training Consultant, ACCH, Bethesda, MD

The Individual Supervisory Plan

Guidelines for Planning Individual Supervision

Another way to organize supervisory plans for individual volunteers is to focus on information needed and behaviors desired. Guiding questions include:

1. What information do I need to know about this individual?

2. What behaviors do I need to assess in this individual?

3. What information do I need to give this individual in:

   ♦ Orientation

   ♦ Making an assignment

4. What information (feedback) do I need from this individual?

5. What are my goals for this individual?

   ♦ ideal

   ♦ satisfactory

6. What behaviors will demonstrate that these goals have been accomplished?

Source: Arlene Kiely, Training Consultant, ACCH, Bethesda, MD

Section Three

Chapter 3.8

Promoting Volunteers

Commentary

IT IS GRATIFYING TO REMEMBER that supervision isn't always centered on problem behaviors! When a volunteer has consistently demonstrated excellent performance, you should consider a promotion. This may be as simple as assigning a volunteer to work with less supervision. It may involve giving a higher level of responsibility. Delegating increased responsibilities to your best volunteers allows you to take care of other needs and expand your program. It is wise to do some anticipatory fantasizing about how you could make use of ideal helpers. You may get them!

Exercise

Improving the Program by Promoting Volunteers

1. In what ways could you improve your program with the help of ideal volunteers?

2. How would you prioritize these visions?

3. Are there volunteers currently capable of taking on a new role or expanded responsibility?

4. What will be required to make this possible?

Source: Arlene Kiely, Training Consultant, ACCH, Bethesda, MD

Section Three

Commentary

DO YOU TAKE THE TIME TO SHARE your visions with your best volunteers? Many of the most capable and flexible volunteers will fill in wherever asked and adapt to the changing needs of the program. If you share your hopes and invite their response, you may find that together you can make improvements. Good volunteers will frequently decide to serve more hours when there is a valuable, specific new service that they can provide. For example, capable volunteers, with guidance, can be quite successful in helping to orient new volunteers, managing a craft cart or story hour, planning a party, or providing special activities for parents or brothers and sisters. Conversely, capable people may leave when they are no longer challenged.

Volunteers may sometimes be enthusiastic about starting a new service that is not feasible in your setting. In this instance, you express appreciation for their creativity and interest and give thoughtful reasons why the program priorities lie elsewhere. It is also wise, with good volunteers, to find out what would make the volunteer experience more satisfying. Given the opportunity, volunteers have been responsible for initiating many innovations in volunteer programs and in developing new services in health agencies.

Chapter 3.9: Improving Performance: Coaching vs. Criticism

ENCOURAGING AND GUIDING VOLUNTEERS to the best possible performance is the ultimate goal of supervision. A good supervisory relationship is based on respectful communication, a process of giving and getting feedback continuously.

Communicating expectations is only the first step in a good supervisory relationship. You must always check to see if the volunteer understands, has questions, or needs clarification. *Communication must also include taking the time to find out what the volunteer is actually experiencing on the job. Your most astute observations can give only a part of the picture.*

One of the best supervisors I know always asks each volunteer, "How did it go today?" She relates, "I'm often surprised by what they tell me was important to them. They may be very pleased or very bothered by something I could not have guessed. By taking just a few minutes to find out, I discover valuable information. It prevents a lot of problems and misunderstanding, and guides me in making the next assignment." It is easy to understand why this supervisor is so successful in keeping volunteers, and rarely has problems. She knows that communication is a two way street, and that taking time daily to ask and to listen promotes good performance and job satisfaction.

But, what does a supervisor do when performance is less than satisfactory? How is it possible to discuss the need for change without offending or discouraging the volunteer?

It is possible to prepare for such situations by practicing in advance.

Before continuing with the specific supervisory situations described in the next chapter, stop and reflect on any internal resistance you may have, as described in the exercise on barriers to supervision. Remember, as that exercise revealed, that there are guidelines to prevent the realization of your worst fears! The same courtesies and considerations offered to children and parents work well in helping volunteers master their adjustment to the volunteer role.

As you plan what you would say and do in each of the practice situations, it would help to keep in mind the following guidelines that enable good supervisors to coach instead of criticize:

Section Three

Guidelines for Coaching Volunteers

1. Communicate acceptance, appreciation, and respect.

2. Keep an open mind! Get the volunteer's input. You seldom have all the puzzle pieces. Feedback is always a two-way street.

3. Focus on the job, not the person. Give information, not criticism. Make your corrections constructive, job specific, and related to specific program goals. Give encouraging, positive reasons for the desired behaviors. This is the essence of coaching versus criticizing.

4. Remember that teaching does not necessarily equal learning; make sure the message has been received.

5. Collaborate on a plan with the volunteer for monitoring performance and for follow-up.

6. Afterward, concentrate on prevention. What have you learned from this situation? What actions could have prevented this occurrence? What will you do to prevent future occurrences? When things go well, how can you duplicate the experience?

Source: Arlene Kiely, Training Consultant, ACCH, Bethesda, MD

Chapter 3.10

Practicing Supervision: Eight Opportunities

Commentary

THE DAILY LIFE OF A SUPERVISOR usually presents abundant opportunities to learn by doing. However, supervisory skills *can* be anticipated and practiced in advance. The following eight situations (on pages 108 to 123) are drawn from actual incidents involving volunteers. Each highlights one or more common supervisory issues. Because the exercises increase in complexity, it is recommended that they be completed in order.

The situations may be reviewed and completed by a single individual. Their use as role plays followed by group discussion provides a much richer educational experience. If you are a lone practitioner, consider organizing a group of at least five people to join you in this professional development exercise or in-service session.

Note: If these incidents do not seem applicable to your work setting, identify real problem situations that do apply. How can you use these as problem-solving opportunities? One way is to use the coaching vs. criticism guidelines to analyze your own situations and think through to solutions. Another method is to take your problem situations to a more experienced supervisor for discussion. A third method is to form a small group that will meet regularly to share real supervisory problem incidents and invite group solutions. The role-play guidelines can also provide a format for discussions of particular situations. Asking for help appropriately is in the finest tradition of mentoring in professional education.

Instructions

For Individual Use: Begin on page 108 and complete each exercise in turn. Each exercise is followed by review questions and commentary.

For Group Use: See the instructions on page 124.

Section Three

Supervisory Opportunity 1

Mary volunteers every Wednesday for four hours. She appears promptly at 10:00 a.m. By the time she arrives, there are already several activities underway. Unfortunately, Mary spends her first 15 minutes chatting with Sara, another volunteer, despite the obvious needs in the playroom. Sara tries to ignore Mary because there is so much to do. You wish Mary would be more alert to the needs for help without waiting for directions from you. You have decided to speak with her about this today.

1. What are the main issues or concerns?

2. What do you need to find out?

3. What will you say to Mary?

4. What do you want Mary to do in the future?

Source: Arlene Kiely, Training Consultant, ACCH, Bethesda, MD

Practicing Supervision: Eight Opportunities

Opportunity 1 Review

This situation highlights the way expectations can influence behavior, and the importance of basic communications.

1. Is the supervisor expecting that the volunteer will automatically perceive what is needed?
2. Is the volunteer expecting to be given specific directions?
3. What about the program needs to be clarified?
   a. the daily schedule
   b. the parameters of the volunteer's initiative
   c. specific activities that the volunteer can do without waiting for the supervisor
   d. the reason for limiting adult conversations to breaks and lunch hour
   e. how a volunteer's early arrival allows time to setup and get an overview of the daily plan

♦ Commentary

Inexperienced supervisors are sometimes hesitant to give even the simplest instruction, yet feel resentful when volunteers are not mind readers. Explaining needs in terms of program goals, while being respectful and appreciative of volunteers' desire to help, creates a sound structure.

Resentments and misunderstanding can grow when supervisors fail to give and get feedback routinely. Dealing with small incidents collaboratively prevents unnecessary problems and is the foundation for a solid working relationship.

♦ Prevention

What can you do to prevent similar occurrences in the future?

Section Three

Supervisory Opportunity 2

Millie is one of your most friendly and dependable volunteers. She comes regularly two mornings a week and instinctively pitches in wherever needed. She has become increasingly attached to Johnny, a toddler who has been here for two months. Lately you have been concerned about signs of over-attachment on Millie's part. She has begun to stay late just to play with Johnny. Today the charge nurse tells you that Millie has started coming in several evenings a week (when you're not present) just to visit with Johnny. How will you handle this?

1. What are the main issues or concerns?

2. What do you need to find out?

3. What will you say to Millie?

4. What do you want Millie to do in the future?

Source: Arlene Kiely, Training Consultant, ACCH, Bethesda, MD

Opportunity 2 Review

This situation highlights the need for continual monitoring of relationships, clarification of supervisory role, and protocols for any deviation from a volunteer's scheduled hours.

1. What are the specific signs and examples of over-attachment? (When discussing behaviors, it is essential to use specific examples.)
2. What is the volunteer's perspective? How did she arrive at the decision to spend extra time with this child?
3. What does this child need? How can the volunteer be guided to a supportive, appropriate relationship?
4. What about family needs, privacy, and support roles of other staff?
5. Program goals to be clarified:
    a. supporting individual children and families
    b. roles of other staff
    c. protocols for serving beyond scheduled hours
    d. importance of monitoring one's own emotional attachments and sharing with supervisor
    e. defining specific ways the volunteer can help the child as well as limitations to her role
    f. possibility that this volunteer might be appropriate for assignment to a one-on-one relationship with this child

♦ Commentary

Supervisors are reluctant to critique anyone as dependable, friendly, and helpful as Millie. A practice of continual feedback prevents the necessity to be critical. In this instance, the social worker's praise of Millie may have helped encourage her to increase her hours. Never underestimate the impact of other staff interactions with volunteers! This emphasizes the importance of clarifying the role of the direct supervisor, to protect volunteers from conflicting messages. Preserving family integrity and privacy is a critical issue. Lack of family visiting can be misinterpreted as evidence of not caring. In fact, we should always assume that families want the best for their children, and do everything possible to support and not supplant their relationship.

On the other hand, many health care agencies are caring for increasing numbers of children who need a regular nurturer. Mature volunteers, with proper guidance, can often fill this role. Some of these individuals have, in fact, become foster or adoptive parents to children with special needs.

♦ Prevention:

What will you do to prevent similar occurrences in the future?

Section Three

Supervisory Opportunity 3

Your schedule has been so hectic for several weeks that the play area is a disaster. You decide to clean the toy cabinets this afternoon. Because you have a regular afternoon volunteer, you feel you can complete the task with an hour's hard work, and then set up for activities. Sally, the afternoon volunteer, usually tells stories and is very popular. However, clean-up is the top priority today. Role play asking Sally's help in cleaning the toy cabinets.

1. What are the main issues or concerns?

2. What do you need to find out?

3. What will you say to Sally?

4. What will you say to Sally if she doesn't want to help clean?

Source: Arlene Kiely, Training Consultant, ACCH, Bethesda, MD

Opportunity 3 Review

This situation highlights the need to prepare volunteers to adapt to changing needs, as well as the need for staff to be appreciative of volunteers' talents.

1. Has the care and maintenance of equipment been taught as a program necessity from the beginning of each volunteer's experience? If not, why not?
2. Has the supervisor encouraged the volunteer to expect that she will always be able to tell stories?
3. Has the supervisor learned about the volunteer as an individual? Family ties? Lifestyle? How does volunteering on a regular basis fit into her overall life? Has the supervisor expressed appreciation for her service and talents?

This is the volunteer perspective which would be assigned to a role player:

You are a regular afternoon volunteer who loves direct interaction with groups of children — the more the better. You're an excellent story teller and look forward to having children respond to your lively interpretations. You have a new story to tell today, and left out-of-town guests at home rather than miss the playroom fun. The disorder in the playroom never bothers you. With your own family, you always felt children should have freedom to enjoy life, and you believe clutter is a sign of a well-used room. You resent being asked to help clean or straighten because you feel it is a waste of your story-telling talents.

♦ Commentary

Performance monitoring frequently involves a redefinition of what is needed to meet changing program needs. Some supervisors playing this role, upon discovering that this volunteer left guests at home, told her to go home and enjoy her guests and made an appointment to review changing needs when the volunteer returns next week. It is also possible that a volunteer who remains inflexible will not be an asset to the program.

♦ Prevention

What will you do to prevent similar occurrences in the future?

Section Three

Supervisory Opportunity 4

You are a nurse on the adolescent unit. Lana is a regular volunteer on Wednesdays. You particularly appreciate her help, since most volunteers prefer to work with younger children. Lana likes to keep busy and never seems to lack for ideas of things to do. This afternoon, David, 15, rejected all Lana's suggestions — to play pinball, go to the library, watch a TV program on magic, do a leathercraft project, help the unit clerk staple papers, play monopoly, or go for a walk. David seemed irritable. Role play your handling of this situation when you and Lana are alone.

1. What are the main issues or concerns?

2. What do you need to find out?

3. What will you say to Lana?

4. What do you want Lana to do in the future?

Source: Arlene Kiely, Training Consultant, ACCH, Bethesda, MD

Opportunity 4 Review

This situation illustrates the importance of monitoring the reactions of the adolescent and the volunteer.

1. Why does the volunteer feel the need to persist despite repeated rejection?
2. What is her role concept?
3. How does the volunteer feel about her lack of success?
4. Can the volunteer be helped to see the value of allowing free choice without feeling personal failure when a choice is rejected?
5. What techniques offer choice and freedom to the child/youth?
6. How can the volunteer's creativity and persistence be channeled appropriately?
7. Can the volunteer's talents and dedication be affirmed so she doesn't feel she did the wrong thing?
8. What is the role of active listening versus constantly keeping children or youth busy?
9. Who will follow up on David's concerns?
10. Are the volunteer's observations about David's status encouraged and appreciated?

♦ Commentary

If regular feedback is not encouraged, volunteers may be reluctant to discuss their frustrations. Thus, opportunities to encourage, redirect, and renew a volunteer's commitment will be missed. Potential opportunities to learn from volunteers' observations will also be missed.

♦ Prevention

What will you do to prevent similar occurrences in the future?

Section Three

Supervisory Opportunity 5

You are the supervisor concerned about the following remarks that Sylvia, a volunteer, made to Mrs. Smith, the parent of another child: "This is Mary, and she's a real sweetheart. Poor thing, she's been here for two months getting treatment for a blood disease. But, even though she's sick, she never complains. I just love working with her, she's my favorite." (Mary is four years old.) What will you say to Sylvia privately?

1. What are the main issues or concerns?

2. What do you need to find out?

3. What will you say to Sylvia?

4. What do you want Sylvia to do in the future?

Source: Arlene Kiely, Training Consultant, ACCH, Bethesda, MD

Opportunity 5 Review

This situation underlines the necessity for absolute confidentiality.

1. Have the guidelines for confidentiality been expressly taught, *practiced*, reviewed, and monitored? If not, why not?
2. Do volunteers understand that confidentiality of information prohibits volunteers giving information to anyone, even a well-known, friendly parent of another child?
3. If confidentiality has been clearly covered, is this volunteer able to observe correct protocols? If not, it may be necessary to give a warning or even consider dismissal.
4. Has the volunteer been taught never to discuss a child in the child's presence?
5. What are the dangers of openly expressing favoritism or pity in the presence of children?
6. How can these vital considerations be taught in advance, to prevent mistakes by well-meaning volunteers?

♦ Commentary

In coaching, give volunteers the benefit of the doubt and reinforce good intentions. This does not preclude making clear the kinds of behaviors that will result in dismissal.

♦ Prevention

What will you do to prevent similar occurrences in the future?

Supervisory Opportunity 6

You are the nurse on the orthopedic unit. You want to talk with Mrs. Ellis, an elderly volunteer, about an incident that occurred at lunchtime. Jason, seven years old, has been in a body cast for two weeks and is getting quite restless. He refused to join a game today. When lunch came, his special-order hot dog was not received. In anger, he threw a puzzle onto the floor and began to cry. Mrs. Ellis said, "You should be ashamed for throwing things and crying at your age." (Assume that you were able to intervene successfully.) How will you discuss this with Mrs. Ellis later?

1. What are the main issues or concerns?

2. What do you need to find out?

3. What will you say to Mrs. Ellis?

4. What do you want Mrs. Ellis to do in the future?

Source: Arlene Kiely, Training Consultant, ACCH, Bethesda, MD

Opportunity 6 Review

This situation highlights the tensions that can result when a volunteer's childrearing practices and expectations conflict with the agency's philosophy of support.

1. What values does the volunteer hold?
2. Can she be helped to see the accumulated stress the child has experienced?
3. Has she been helped to understand the special functions of play in the hospital?
4. What appropriate preventive, interventive comments can she be taught to help reduce stress and support the child?
5. Can she be helped to see the negative effects of shaming a child? And the positive benefits of listening for feelings and empathizing with frustrations?

♦ Commentary

It is important to respect the successful child rearing experience of volunteers and not imply that differing family strategies are wrong. Many adults were reared in a more authoritarian era where "children should be seen and not heard." Others experienced a more permissive upbringing with little structure.

It is essential that the values and philosophy of the agency program be explained in advance, using examples of specific situations, the needs of children, and the reasons that particular approaches are desirable. New behaviors and communication skills can be learned, especially where they are modelled and practiced in advance.

♦ Prevention

What will you do to prevent similar occurrences in the future?

Section Three

Supervisory Opportunity 7

You have been concerned about 6-year-old Mike who has been hospitalized here for three days and has refused to come to the playroom. He is withdrawn, looks sad, but has shared his feelings with no one. You ask Ann, a calm and regular volunteer, to take in a few books and see if a story would be welcomed. Half an hour later when you go to Mike's room you can see he has been crying for some time. However, he is wiping his nose, has stopped crying, and is preparing to come to the playroom with Ann. What will you say to Ann later today when you are alone together.

1. What are the main issues or concerns?

2. What do you need to find out?

3. What will you say to Ann?

Source: Arlene Kiely, Training Consultant, ACCH, Bethesda, MD

Opportunity 7 Review

This is not a trick situation! It highlights the importance of catching volunteers at exemplary behaviors, offering praise, and finding out what can be learned from them.

1. What did the volunteer do to reach this child? Since you can only find out by asking, the volunteer's description of this situation is included here:

You are a regular volunteer with lots of experience with children. Today the nurse suggests you take some books in to Mike, a withdrawn six-year old who has refused to come to the playroom since admission three days ago. When you went into the room, Mike turned his head away from you. You sat down and said, "Sometimes people get awfully tired of being in the hospital." Mike looked at you and said, "I want to go home!" You responded, "I *know* you do! That's just what we want, too. We want to help you get well so you can go home. Who's waiting for you at home?" At this point, Mike began to cry and tell you about his parents, his new baby sister, and his dog. You listened, allowed him to cry, and said, "I'll bet they can hardly wait 'till you get home." When his crying subsided and he seemed to feel better, you said, "Would you like to go with me to see what's happening in the playroom? We can always come back if you don't want to stay." Naturally, you're feeling very good that Mike *did* go with you to the playroom!

2. What special sensitivities does her behavior illustrate?
3. Could this volunteer help teach other volunteers?

◆ Commentary

Just as good teachers expect to learn from students, good supervisors expect to learn from volunteers. This situation highlights the importance of "catching good behaviors" and offering praise. Supervision involves more than correction. Praising, encouraging, and finding out what you can learn from sensitive volunteers is also important. A good supervisor will be appreciative and not threatened by a volunteer's success, and know how to make use of exceptional skills.

Section Three

Supervisory Opportunity 8

You are the child life specialist, concerned about Jack, a college sophomore who assists on your unit three afternoons a week this summer. He has lots of energy and relates well to children, but is headstrong. The charge nurse tells you that Jack came in early this morning and took pictures of two children without your knowledge or the consent of the children or families. The nurse informed Jack that picture taking is against hospital policy. You know that volunteer orientation clearly covers this policy, verbally and in writing. Furthermore, you reinforced the policy just last week by insisting that Jack put away his camera. What will you do?

1. What are the main issues or concerns?

2. Is there anything else you need to know?

3. What will you say and do?

Source: Arlene Kiely, Training Consultant, ACCH, Bethesda, MD

Opportunity 8 Review

This situation tests whether or not a supervisor can recognize evidence of serious infractions and take action for immediate dismissal.

Unfortunately, some people reviewing this situation are tempted to bend over backwards and give this volunteer one more chance! This is worse than a simple "triumph of hope over experience."

- *Failure to dismiss this volunteer will predictably result in future problems, perhaps liability.* Why?
- This volunteer has had *three* specific opportunities to *learn* and *practice* the protocols for confidentiality.
- *His behavior clearly demonstrates he does not respect the protocol, has no intention of observing it, and will, in fact, make every effort to circumvent it.*

It is foolhardy and irresponsible to ignore this evidence. For the protection of children, families, and the agency's reputation, this volunteer must be dismissed immediately. Furthermore, he should be required to turn over the film negatives to the agency.

♦ Commentary

Dismissing volunteers is not an easy task. Guidelines for dismissing volunteers are essential. This information is covered in Chapter 1.10. If you have not already read Chapter 1.10, Dismissing Volunteers, review it now. Then return to Chapter 3.12 for a review of supervisory skills and a personal action plan.

♦ Prevention

What can you do to prevent this kind of situation in the future?

Section Three

Group Instructions for Supervisory Opportunities

♦ Leader's Advance Preparation:

1. Complete the individual exercises beginning on page 108. Make notes on any issues overlooked.
2. Read the volunteer role descriptions for each situation on page 126. Each adds complexity to the situation.

Materials Needed

1. Photocopy handouts for role players:
   - For eight supervisory roles, copy the pages that describe each supervisory situation. (Do not include the commentary/review pages.)
   - Copy the corresponding volunteer roles on page 126 and cut apart for eight volunteers.
2. Make an overhead, or photocopies, of the Guidelines for Coaching on page 106.
3. Make an overhead, or photocopies, of the Roleplay Observer's Worksheet on page 128.

♦ Leading the Group — Total time required: 1½ Hours

1. **Prepare the Group** — Explain that role play is an opportunity to practice supervisory skills among colleagues and to develop a personal action plan based on shared learning. Explain that role players need not know all the answers, and that observers are not critiquing individuals, but are looking for ways to improve performance.

2. **Establish the agenda**
   - We will do eight role plays.
   - While players are preparing their roles, observers will reflect on how they might approach each situation.
   - Role play may be concluded by players or the leader.
   - Observers will comment and then players will be asked to comment.

3. **Review the Guidelines for Coaching.**

4. **Say that observers will be asked to identify and discuss:**
   - the central issues or concerns;
   - the supervisor's coaching techniques;
   - volunteer's concerns and perceptions; and
   - prevention strategies.

5. **Prepare Role Players** — Take each role play in turn. Ask for two volunteers, or assign roles. Give each role player a photocopied descrip-

Practicing Supervision: Eight Opportunities

tion *of their role only*. Players must not read each other's roles. Give each player a few moments alone outside the room to consider the written directions.

6. **Give Worksheets to Observers** — While players are preparing their roles elsewhere, read aloud the supervisor's description for that situation. Have observers reflect on what they would do as the supervisor.

7. **Role Play** — When players are ready, begin. Each role play should be brief, and conclude as soon as either player or leader feels it is appropriate.

8. **Discuss Each Role Play** — Ask the observers:

   - What are the central issues?
   - What were the issues for the volunteer?
   - What did the supervisor do that was helpful? What did the supervisor do to:
     - communicate acceptance and respect?
     - get volunteer's input?
     - coach instead of criticize?
     - give positive reasons for desired behaviors?
     - collaborate with volunteer on follow-up?
   - What else could the supervisor have done to:
     - communicate acceptance and respect?
     - get volunteer's input?
     - coach instead of criticize?
     - give positive reasons for desired behaviors?
     - collaborate with volunteer on follow-up?
   - **What could be done to prevent future occurrences with this or other volunteers?**
   - Next, ask the supervisor and volunteer what made the counseling session easy or difficult. You may decide at this point to have the volunteer read their instructions to the group to see if any important input was missed. Ask players what prevention strategies they would use in the future. Be sure to thank them for taking part and helping the group.

Section Three

Eight Supervisory Opportunities: Volunteers' Roles

Give each role player a photocopied description *of their role only.*

Situation 1: You have been a regular child life volunteer for several months. You come promptly at 10:00 a.m. and stay faithfully until 2:00 p.m. You enjoy working with the children and also visiting with Sara, another volunteer who is about your age. You have a great deal of respect for the child life worker, and feel that "a child life specialist's playroom is her castle." You feel that the child life worker is the "boss" of the program, and you don't like to get involved in anything until she tells you exactly what she wants you to do. So, you usually visit with Sara (who arrives earlier) until the supervisor has time to give you a job to do. Role play your response to the child life specialist's conference with you now.

Situation 2: You are an enthusiastic, devoted volunteer on the toddler unit. Children respond well to your warm, friendly manner and volunteering gives you a real sense of purpose and belonging. You regret you never married or had children, and sometimes wonder if you should adopt a child. Johnny, a particularly appealing toddler, has become your special favorite. You've started staying late to give him extra time, because his family hardly ever visits. You suspect many family problems, because one social worker told you she's glad Johnny has some consistent attention. You've started coming in several evenings a week, when the child life specialist isn't there, just to play with Johnny. Role play your reactions to the child life specialist's conference.

Situation 3: You are a regular afternoon volunteer who loves direct interaction with groups of children — the more the better. You're an excellent story teller and look forward to having children respond to your lively interpretations. You have a new story to tell today, and left out-of-town guests at home rather than miss the playroom fun. The disorder in the playroom never bothers you. With your own family, you always felt children should have freedom to enjoy life, and you believe clutter is a sign of a well-used room. You resent being asked to help clean or straighten because you feel it is a waste of your story-telling talents. Role play your reactions to the child life specialist's conference.

Situation 4: You are Lana, an enthusiastic volunteer on the adolescent unit. When you see teenagers lying around, you try your best to interest them in some kind of activity. You are creative and persistent in thinking up things to do. You frequently will get a response from a teenager who rejects your first few ideas. You hate to see kids moping and depressed when activity can do them so much good. Today you feel like a failure. You were unable to dream up anything David, 15, wanted to do. You are very disappointed and wonder if you did any good today. Role play Lana and respond to the nurse.

Situation 5: You are Sylvia, a dedicated volunteer. You are amazed at how sweet some children can be even when they're sick. Four-year-old Mary is one of your favorites. You have worked with her for two months and have never seen any family members visit. You've gotten to know several other parents who come to visit their children. Mrs. Smith seems especially nice. Today when Mrs. Smith asked you what was wrong with Mary, you told her that Mary has a blood disease. You also told her that Mary is your favorite. Role play Sylvia's response to the supervisor.

Practicing Supervision: Eight Opportunities

Situation 6: You are Mrs. Ellis, an elderly volunteer. You have raised 7 children and 11 grandchildren. You love coming to the hospital to help out on the orthopedic floor. There are many activities and sometimes you think these children don't appreciate all the things that are available. Today you tried working with Jason, a seven-year old who is usually very polite. You offered him a game but he refused. When the right lunch didn't come, he threw his puzzle on the floor. You don't think children should be allowed to throw tantrums and treat a nice playroom that way. Jason started to cry, and you said, "You should be ashamed, throwing things and crying at your age." Role play Mrs. Ellis and her response to the nurse.

Situation 7: You are a regular volunteer with lots of experience with children. Today the nurse suggests you take some books in to Mike, a withdrawn six-year old who has refused to come to the playroom since admission three days ago. **Reveal the following information *only* if you are asked:** When you went into the room, Mike turned his head away from you. You sat down and said, "Sometimes people get awfully tired of being in the hospital." Mike looked at you and said, "I want to go home!" You responded, "I *know* you do! That's just what we want, too. We want to help you get well so you can go home. Who's waiting for you at home?" At this point, Mike began to cry and tell you about his parents, his new baby sister, and his dog. You listened, allowed him to cry, and said, "I'll bet they can hardly wait 'till you get home." When his crying subsided and he seemed to feel better, you said, "Would you like to go with me to see what's happening in the playroom? We can always come back if you don't want to stay." Naturally, you're feeling very good that Mike *did* go with you to the playroom! Role play your response to the supervisor's conference later when you are alone together.

Situation 8: You are Jack, a college sophomore volunteering three days a week during the summer. You completed the volunteer orientation but you think some of the rules are too strict. For example, you think it is foolish not to be allowed to take pictures of kids. Kids enjoy posing for cameras. You want to have some pictures to illustrate a paper you are writing for a psychology class. Last week the child life specialist wouldn't allow you to take pictures and made you put your camera away. This morning you came early, and took a few pictures anyway before the child life specialist came. However, a nurse caught you and made you put your camera away, and reported you to the child life specialist. Role play your defense.

Source: Arlene Kiely, Training Consultant, ACCH, Bethesda, MD

Section Three

Role-Play Observers' Worksheet

If you were the supervisor in this situation what would you do?

1. What are the issues? (**Analysis**)

2. What other information do you need? (**Input**)

3. What program goals need to be clarified? (**Information**)

4. What do you want the volunteer to DO in the future? (**Behavior**)

5. How will you communicate? (**Information and Behavior**)

6. What will you do to prevent a recurrence? (**Prevention**)

Source: Arlene Kiely, Training Consultant, ACCH, Bethesda, MD

Chapter 3.11

Conclusion: Supervisory Skills Review and Action Plan

SUPERVISION IS CHALLENGING because it requires an open mind, a willingness to assume responsibility, and enthusiasm for working and learning with others. The principles and practices covered throughout this section on supervision should enable you to take advantage of opportunities for learning in your setting. Taking responsibility for your own continuing education as a supervisor will require ongoing reflection on what is needed, a specific plan of action, and a deliberate use of resources. With experience, this process becomes habitual.

The list of What Good Supervisors Do, which follows, summarizes the supervisory development topics covered in this section and elsewhere in this manual. Use this list for a personal review. Then, complete the Supervisory Development Action Plan for your continuing education. Good luck!

We hope this manual has been helpful to you, your program, and the children and families you serve. You can help ACCH by completing and returning the publication evaluation form, Appendix C, pages C2 to C4.

What Good Supervisors Do

(A summary of supervisory development topics covered in *Volunteers in Child Health: Management, Selection, Training, and Supervision.*)

1. Understand the purpose and process of supervision. (Chapters 3.1, 3.2)

2. Identify barriers to effective supervision. (Chapters 3.3, 3.6)

3. Write volunteer job descriptions. (Chapter 1.4)

4. Review job description with volunteer, relating performance expectations to program goals. (Chapter 3.4)

5. Communicate expectations clearly in terms of what is always expected, what is optional, and what behaviors are prohibited. (Chapter 3.4)

6. Welcome volunteers and orient to immediate environment, team members, and usual daily routines. (Chapter 2.1, 3.4)

Section Three

7. Asses individual volunteer's capabilities; comfort level; ability to interact appropriately with children, parents, and staff; judgment; and commitment. (Chapters 3.5, 3.7, 3.8)

8. Give an appropriate first assignment. (Chapter 3.5)

9. Have an assignment ready for volunteers each time they come; teach how they are to proceed in the supervisor's absence. (Chapters 3.4, 3.5)

10. Work closely with volunteers to model appropriate behaviors and observe readiness for new assignments or independent performance. (Chapter 3.8)

11. Get feedback each day by asking the volunteer, "How did it go today?" Discuss and plan future work accordingly. (Chapter 3.9)

12. Give feedback as soon as possible, in private. (Chapters 3.9, 3.10)

13. Coach performance instead of criticizing. Relate desired behaviors to program goals. Agree upon a plan for follow-up. (Chapter 3.9, 3.10)

14. Deal with serious problems without delay. (Chapters 3.10)

15. Express praise and appreciation immediately. (Chapters 1.9, 3.10)

16. Include outstanding volunteers in problem solving and the development of new services. (Chapter 3.8)

17. Plan special occasions to recognize and reward volunteers at least once a year. (Chapter 1.9)

18. Do an exit interview when volunteers leave. (Chapter 1.10)

19. Dismiss volunteers when necessary. (Chapter 1.11)

20. Never miss an opportunity to learn from mistakes! Analyze problem situations to discover prevention strategies. (Chapter 3.10, 1.11)

Conclusion: Supervisory Skills Review and Action Plan

Supervisory Development Action Plan

EVALUATE YOUR SKILL and your needs in each of the following areas. List the resources available to you and a timetable for your personal action plan in each of the areas that need attention.

	Doing Well	Need Work	Resources Available	Action Plan
Identifying Barriers to Supervision				
Communicating Expectations				
Relating Behaviors to Program Goals				
Understanding Personal Preferences				
Assessment of Volunteers				
Supervisory Plan				
Getting Feedback				
Coaching vs. Criticizing				
Promoting Volunteers				
Dismissing Volunteers				
Recognizing and Rewarding				

Source: Arlene Kiely, Training Consultant, ACCH, Bethesda, MD

Section Three

Appendix A: Administrative Resources

Table of Contents

Job Description Worksheet	A2
Sample Job Description	A3
Sample Application Form	A5
Sample Time Sheet	A7
Sample Policies and Procedures for Volunteers	A8
Sample Exit Interview Questionnaire	A10
Guidelines for Entertainers	A11
Sample Toy Brochure	A13

NOTE: These materials have been generously shared for this publication. Sources must be credited when materials are photocopied, adapted, or used in any way.

Appendix A

Job Description Worksheet

What do you want a volunteer working with you to do *always...sometimes...never*? List these specific functions below:

Always:

Sometimes:

Never:

How will you make these expectations clear in the job description?

Source: Arlene Kiely, Training Consultant, ACCH, Bethesda, MD

Administrative Resources

Sample Job Description

Evening/Weekend Volunteers Who Work Directly With Children

Job Description: Evening/weekend volunteers are prepared to function independently providing play, recreational, and supportive activities to children and families on patient care units. They serve at bedsides, in playrooms, and in isolation.

Hours: Evening/weekend volunteers serve a minimum of two hours on the same day each week. (Evening: any two hours after 4:00 p.m. Weekend: any two hours from 8:30 a.m. to 10:00 p.m.) Regular hours, appropriate to the unit, are scheduled with the PM/WK coordinator.

Ongoing Responsibilities:

1. To assess the needs of children and families for volunteer support.
2. To plan and implement age-appropriate play, recreational, and supportive activities which normalize the hospital environment for children and families.
3. To promote socialization among children and families through such activities as group play and group meals.
4. To assist children with meals as needed.
5. To seek information from staff, when necessary, about a child's special needs and/or restrictions (such as special diet, activity level allowed, etc.).
6. To report unusual occurrences to child's nurse immediately.
7. To know and uphold hospital and volunteer policies at all times.
8. To adapt to changing needs of the unit and hospital.

Optional Responsibilities:

1. Volunteers may transport a child within the hospital with permission from the child's nurse.
2. Volunteers may remain with a child to provide comfort and support during medical or nursing procedures.
3. Volunteers may change diapers at their discretion.
4. Volunteers may work with children in isolation as needed.

Limitations to Information/Activity:

1. Volunteers do not perform medical or nursing procedures (such as tube feedings, baths, dressing changes) of any kind.
2. Volunteers do not have access to patient charts.
3. Volunteers preserve family privacy by refraining from questioning staff, children, or families about a child's diagnosis.
4. Volunteers do not discuss child's medical condition unless child or family initiates discussion.
5. Volunteers do not give medical advice, but refer all medical questions to the appropriate staff promptly.
6. Volunteers confine their role to the hospital setting.

Supervision:

Evening/weekend volunteers are trained, placed, scheduled, and supervised by PM/WK Volunteer Coordinator. While working on patient care units, they are directly accountable to the nursing staff and report on and off to the nurse.

Adapted from: Volunteer Services, Children's National Medical Center, Washington, D.C.

Administrative Resources

Children's National Medical Center.

Sample Application Form

VOLUNTEER SERVICE APPLICATION

(An Equal Opportunity Program)

▶ Name: _____

▶ Address: _____

_____

▶ Home Telephone: _____ Business Telephone: _____

▶ In case of emergency, notify: _____ Relationship: _____

Work Telephone: _____ Home Telephone: _____

▶ Please circle age group: 16-18   19-40   41-60   Over 60

▶ **EMPLOYMENT:**

Employer: _____

Position: _____ Hours: _____

▶ **EDUCATION:**

I have completed: ☐ High School ☐ Some College ☐ College ☐ Graduate School

☐ Other: _____ ☐ Degree or Major: _____

I am now studying at: _____ Year: _____

☐ Full-time   ☐ Part-time   Subject/Major: _____

List courses relating to your volunteer interest: _____

_____
_____

▶ **AVAILABILITY:**

I would be able to volunteer: ☐ Evenings ☐ Weekends ☐ Weekdays

Beginning (Month/Year): _____

▶ **INTERESTS:**

How did you become interested in volunteering at Children's?

What would you most like to do here as a volunteer?

Source: Volunteer Services, Children's National Medical Center, Washington, D.C.

OFFICE USE
Received: _____
Card Sent: _____

Last Name: _____
First Name: _____

A5

(continued)   *Appendix A*

Would you prefer to volunteer -

▶ **Directly with children**
(Volunteer must be over 18)

☐ Patient Care   ☐ Pre-Surgical Orientation
☐ Family Library
☐ Home Support/Hospice
☐ Other: _____

▶ **Other service areas:**

☐ Information Desk   ☐ Gift Shop
☐ Blood Donor Center   ☐ Clerical Support
☐ Clinic   ☐ Library
☐ Other: _____

▶ **EXPERIENCE:**

Please list previous volunteer experience *(organization, location, dates, hours served, and what you did):* _____

_____

List experience you have had with children *(including your own)* and age groups:

_____

_____

List any other experiences or skills related to your volunteer interests: _____

_____

List organizations or clubs in which you are active: _____

_____

▶ **HEALTH:**

Is there any health reason which might limit your ability to volunteer? ☐ YES ☐ NO

If yes, please explain: _____

▶ **REFERENCES:**

Please print names and addresses of three persons we may contact who have known you for more than one year *(excluding relatives or roommates).*

Name: _____ Phone: _____
Address: _____
Name: _____ Phone: _____
Address: _____
Name: _____ Phone: _____
Address: _____

▶ *I understand volunteers must be at least 15 years of age, agree to serve a regular placement of at least 100 hours in a calendar year, and submit a health form before beginning volunteer service.*

▶ Signature: _____ Date: _____

▶ Please return to: Volunteer Services Department, Children's National Medical Center
111 Michigan Avenue, N.W., Washington, D.C. 20010-2970, (202) 745-2062

Sample Time Sheet

VOLUNTEER TIME AND RECORD SHEET

NAME _____
HOME PHONE _____
ASSIGNMENT _____
ADDRESS _____
BUSINESS PHONE _____
COMMITMENT _____

E = EXCUSED   V = ON VACATION   A = ABSENT WITHOUT CALLING   I = INACTIVE

	1	2	3	4	5	6	7	8	9	10	11	12	13	14	15	16	17	18	19	20	21	22	23	24	25	26	27	28	29	30	31	TOTAL MONTH	TOTAL YEAR
JAN																																	
FEB																																	
MAR																																	
APR																																	
MAY																																	
JUN																																	
JUL																																	
AUG																																	
SEP																																	
OCT																																	
NOV																																	
DEC																																	

Source: Volunteer Services, Children's National Medical Center, Washington, D.C.

Appendix A

Sample Policies and Procedures for Volunteers

Volunteer Services: Children's National Medical Center welcomes qualified volunteers to serve a regular assignment supplementing the services of salaried staff throughout the hospital. No hospital or departmental policy or procedure shall discriminate on the basis of race, creed, color, sex, national origin, or handicap.

Availability: Hospital volunteers are required to commit themselves for one year of service, two to four hours per week. In special circumstances a commitment of 100 hours of concentrated service may be accepted.

Limitation to Volunteered Services:

Legally, a volunteer may not practice his/her profession (R.N., M.D., art therapist, etc.) while working as a volunteer. Volunteers are not allowed to perform any medical or nursing procedures.

Age Requirements: All volunteers must be at least 16 years old. Volunteers must be at least 18 years old to work on patient units, after 5:00 p.m., or on weekends.

Selection: Volunteers must successfully complete all application, orientation, and training requirements before placement.

Health Form: No volunteer may begin assignment until a current health form is received. D.C. law requires that health forms be updated annually.

Placement: All placements and reassignments are made by the Volunteer Office in accordance with hospital needs, volunteer skills, and availability.

Attendance: Volunteers who must be absent should notify the Volunteer Office and supervisor by 9:30 a.m. (weekday volunteers), or 4:30 p.m. (evening). Evening/weekend volunteers who are unable to reach the office should call the following work day.

Identification and Security:

1. Every volunteer must wear his/her uniform and name badge while on duty in the hospital.
2. Volunteers must sign in and out on each day of assignment.
3. Valuables should be locked in the Volunteer Office lockers. Locker keys should be pinned inside uniform pocket and returned to the lock at the end of each day of service.
4. Volunteer's guests must report to the Volunteer Office. Guests may only visit the lobby area, snack bar, and cafeteria.
5. Security guards are on duty around the clock. Call extension _____ for escorts to cars, lost and found, theft or robbery.

Conduct:

1. Volunteers are expected to know and uphold the hospital philosophy and all regulations regarding safety, confidentiality, and acceptable conduct.
2. Volunteers do not have access to patient charts.
3. Volunteers must keep in confidence any information they may receive about a patient.
4. Volunteers cannot use a camera in the hospital.
5. Solicitation or distribution of literature on hospital property is prohibited at all times.

Termination: At any time, the Director of Volunteers may terminate the placement of a volunteer for unsatisfactory performance and/or failure to comply with hospital or departmental regulations.

Accidents and Injuries: Any accident or injury, no matter how small, which involves patients, parents, volunteers, or visitors must be reported immediately to the on-site supervisor and the Director of Volunteers.

Benefits:

1. Parking — Volunteers receive complimentary parking in the hospital parking lot during their hours of volunteer service.
2. Cafeteria — Volunteers may eat in the hospital cafeteria between 7:00 a.m. and 7:00 p.m. Volunteers wearing the uniform and name badge are granted a discount on cafeteria meals.
3. Tax Deductions — Volunteers may deduct from their income tax:
    a. Those cost of their uniforms; and
    b. Transportation expenses incurred in rendering volunteered services.
4. Training — Volunteers will receive orientation and training prior to placement. Follow-up and in-service training opportunities will be available throughout the year.

Source: Volunteer Services, Children's National Medical Center, Washington, D.C.

Appendix A

Sample Exit Interview Questionnaire

We are always striving to improve the performance of our volunteer management system. Please be as complete and honest as you can in answering the following questions — all of the information collected will be kept strictly confidential, but it will be utilized to ensure that others who volunteer will receive the best possible treatment.

How long did you volunteer with us?

Types of volunteer positions held:

1.

2.

Reason you are leaving (check all that apply):

- ❏ Job accomplished
- ❏ Moving to a new location
- ❏ Didn't like the jobs I was given
- ❏ Need a change
- ❏ Other time commitments
- ❏ Other:

What did you like best about volunteering with us?

_____
_____
_____
_____

What suggestions would you make for future volunteers?

_____
_____
_____
_____

Overall, how would you rate your experience in volunteering with us?

TERRIBLE			AVERAGE			GREAT
1	2	3	4	5	6	7

Please return this form to:

Source: Child Life Department, The Johns Hopkins Children's Center, Baltimore, Maryland

Administrative Resources

Guidelines for Entertainers

WE APPRECIATE YOUR INTEREST in volunteering your talents to entertain. Because we wish for a good experience for children, families, staff members, and performers alike, we have developed the following guidelines. Please review them carefully before you return, and don't hesitate to call in advance of your scheduled performance if you have any questions.

Your performance is scheduled for _____. Please arrive promptly at _____ (location) by _____ (time). To allow maximum enjoyment, your performance should begin at and end by _____.

Costumes: Ask about the location for changing into any costume, to avoid attracting attention when you arrive.

Content: As we have discussed, entertainment for children should not contain violence, weapons, or any suggestion of physical harm or death. As a nonsectarian agency, we must also avoid religious content, which might be different from the beliefs of some families represented here.

Humor: Please avoid using health or medical humor of any kind. Young children can misunderstand a great deal in a medical setting and mistake humor for something that might really happen to them.

Gifts, prizes, favors, and refreshments: In general, it is better that these items be eliminated. Please check with staff in advance about the kinds of items that meet safety and medical requirements, and are appropriate to the age and condition of the children. When items have been approved, it is essential that you assure that there are more than enough to go around for the children and any brothers and sisters who might be present. A wonderful performance can be ruined if a single child is left out when tokens are distributed.

Competitions and contests: These are to be avoided. Any suggestion of rankings can increase anxiety when children are feeling vulnerable.

Helpful Hints for the Day of Performance:

1. You will be met by an official guide who will take you to the area where you may change costume, and then to the area selected for performance. Your guide will be familiar with any special circumstances and will introduce you to the appropriate staff. Take your cues from your guide, and wait to be introduced before initiating conversation with children.

2. Please enter only those rooms and areas indicated by your guide.

3. Very young children are frequently suspicious of strangers. This natural fear may be heightened in an environment which is not home. Approach children slowly. Let the guide introduce you. If children move confidently toward you, this indicates they are ready to interact.

Appendix A

4. Young children are frequently confused by masks and costumes. Let the child's reactions be your guide.
5. Some children participate best by observing.
6. Please do not pick up any child unless your guide indicates it is acceptable. It can be frightening to be picked up by a stranger. Occasionally, there may be medical reasons why a particular child should not be picked up.
7. Please do not ask information about the diagnosis or condition of any child. This is confidential information and must be respected at all times, just as you would rightfully expect this agency to preserve your own child's or family's right to privacy if your child were receiving service here.
8. No photographs of any child may be taken without the signed consent of the child's parents or guardian. This rule must be strictly observed. Agency staff members must use the agency's photographic release form in advance. Similarly, no child's name, or any information whatsoever about a child and family, may be used in any publicity without the parent's signed consent obtained in advance by agency staff.
9. It is not unusual for people to regress when not feeling well. Children may revert to an earlier stage of development, and reflect this in their behavior. This is normal.
10. Children may not always show their appreciation and enjoyment directly. If you receive smiles, laughs, and direct thank you's from the children, we will be pleased. Remember, however, that some children who make no immediate response will talk about an event for many days afterward.

We trust that these general guidelines will help prepare you for this experience. We thank you for your interest in sharing your time and talents with us. If these guidelines have raised other questions, please call _____ at _____ .

Source: Arlene Kiely, Training Consultant, ACCH, Bethesda, MD

Sample Toy Brochure

Holidays, Toys, Children and You!

Hospitalized children need toys for play year round, but especially at holidays.

Toys donated by community friends keep playrooms supplied and help make special celebrations possible. Donated decorations add holiday cheer to all playrooms and patient care areas.

May your thoughtfulness to others return in good measure to you and yours this season and throughout the year.

Santa visits the bedside of each child on Christmas morning. Hospital staff spend several weeks before Christmas carefully selecting personalized gifts for the children. You and your group can help by following our guidelines.

Popular Favorites for All Ages

Infants: Crib mobiles • Music boxes/rattles • Cradle gyms • Soft rubber dolls • Fisher Price toys • Infant mirrors

Toddlers: Push/pull/talking toys • Wooden puzzles • Musical toys/boxes • Water toys • Fisher Price toys/games • Wonderful waterfuls • Dolls (especially black) • Fisher Price Medical Kit • Non-toxic Play Doh • Tonka, vehicles

School Age: Board games (i.e. Candy Land) • Puzzles • Craft/paint/model sets • Etch-a-Sketch • Crayons (small boxes) • Art supplies • Superhero dolls • Speak and Spell • Activity books

Adolescents: Shiny mobiles • Playing cards/puzzle books • Games (i.e. Mastermind) • Advanced craft & paint supplies • Blank tape cassettes • Grooming kits & supplies (perfume, after-shave, etc.) • Battery powered games

If you are considering donating a large toy or recreational item please call the volunteer office staff first for guidelines.

Please Remember

Yes, toys are needed year-round for all age groups. Our patients range in age from a few hours old to nineteen years old.

Visiting policies: Because our patients are acutely ill, we are unable to allow donors to deliver gifts or give parties directly to the children.

Only new toys are used at Christmas. Please deliver toys before December 14 to allow staff time for personalized selections. Please save good used toys for delivery after January 1.

Deliver donations to the Volunteer Office weekdays between 9:00 a.m. and 4:00 p.m. If you must deliver another time, please attach your name, address and list your donation.

Please do not wrap gifts. Safety regulations require even labelled gifts to be checked for appropriateness. Wrapping paper, ribbons, tape and tags are most welcome.

Toy safety guidelines protect children. Before you select gifts, please make sure they meet our toy safety guidelines.

Holiday decorations are used throughout the hospital. All must be flame proof, non-electrical and unbreakable.

Christmas: Small artificial trees are welcome. Fire regulation prohibit live trees.

Donated Santa suits can be worn by hospital staff.

Small stockings filled with one or two safe, small toys and a few commercially wrapped candies are excellent.

All edible goodies must be commercially made and wrapped. Lollipops and small candy canes are excellent. Holiday placemats (13 1/2" x 18"), and decorated cups we can fill are appreciated. Please do not use straight pins, toothpicks, sharp or unsafe items in tray favors.

Please remember, we cannot display denominational or religious materials.

Toy Safety Guidelines

✦ Stuffed toys can only be used if they are filled with fabric or solid foam. No shredded foam, small pellets, or beans can be used as filler. Avoid toys with detachable parts (like button eyes) which can be removed and swallowed or inhaled.

✦ Fire regulations forbid electrical, spark-producing, or friction-producing toys.

✦ Toys should be sturdy. Avoid toys which can break and leave sharp edges. No toys should be made of glass or brittle plastic.

✦ Avoid toys with sharp edges or protrusions which can be poked into eyes.

✦ Painted toys should be non-toxic.

✦ Toys should not have parts which can pinch fingers or toes or catch hair.

✦ Any glue or paint in craft kits must be non-toxic.

✦ Toys should be in new or almost new condition.

✦ Toys with numerous small parts which require close supervision are not appropriate.

✦ "Humorous" medical toys and games cause fears and misconceptions and are therefore inappropriate.

Source: Adapted from the attractive, illustrated 11" x 14" self-mailer used by Volunteer Services, Children's National Medical Center, Washington, DC (Note: Original stat not available.)

Appendix A

Appendix B

Orientation and Training Resources

Table of Contents

Personal Orientation Checklist	B2
Safety Orientation Checklist	B3
Confidentiality: A Volunteer's Obligations	B8
Confidentiality and Privacy Exercise	B9
Confidentiality and Privacy: What Volunteers Need to Know	B10
Infection Control	B12
The Psychological Impact of Illness and Hospitalization Upon the Child — Infancy to Twelve Years	B16
Family-Centered Care	B29
Guidelines for Supporting Families	B31
Reflections on Child Development	B33
Individuality of Temperament	B36
Understanding Personal Preferences	B42
Observing and Playing with Children	B44
Self-Orientation: Play in This Setting	B51
Exercise: What is Play?	B53
List of Suggested Play Materials	B55
Exercise: Play Activities Review	B61
Planning Age-Appropriate Play: Volunteer Exercise	B62
Planning Age-Appropriate Play: Instructor's Guide	B64
Guidelines for Expressive Arts with Children	B67
Guidelines for Interacting with Children and Adolescents in Health Care Settings	B68
Some Helpful Techniques in Managing Children's Behavior	B69
Limits and Limit Setting	B70
What Will You Say or Do?	B71
Medical Play	B72
Exercise: The Habit of Reflection	B75
Self Evaluation and Action Plan	B77

NOTE: These materials have been generously shared for this publication. Sources must be credited when materials are photocopied, adapted, or used in any way.

Appendix B

NAME: _____ Date Completed _____

Personal Orientation Checklist

Instructions: Date each item as you learn the information or procedures required.

Date Completed

1. Where to sign in _____
2. Where to store my belongings _____
3. Restroom locations _____
4. Telephone _____
5. Food service _____
6. Parking _____
7. Public transportation or taxi _____
8. Building security _____
9. Emergency procedures: _____
   — fire _____
   — accident _____
   — medical emergency _____
   — disaster _____
10. Confidentiality _____
11. Privacy _____
12. Safety _____
13. Absenteeism _____
14. Review of my job description _____
15. Health requirements completed _____
16. Days and hours I will serve _____
17. Supervisor's name _____
18. Alternate supervisor _____

Checklist Reviewed with Supervisor: _____
                                              Signature

Volunteers in Child Health:

Orientation and Training Resources

Safety Orientation Checklist

> **ALWAYS REMEMBER**
> Before working with any child, ask staff these questions:
> 1. Are there any activity restrictions?
> 2. Are there any dietary restrictions?
> 3. Is there anything else I need to know?

Name: _____

Dates Completed

	Discussion	Practice

Holding and positioning infants
- supporting neck
- cradling close to body for security
- proper positioning for infants unable to sit without support

Crib and Bed Safety
- how to raise and lower side rails — crib
- never leaving side rails down
- keeping safety pins closed and out of reach
- purpose and use of safety tents and nets
- mobile safety
- how to raise and lower siderails — bed
- how to raise and lower sections of bed
- not raising bed sections without staff consent
- how to assist an older child to get out of bed

Management, Selection, Training & Supervision

Appendix B

Dates Completed

	Discussion	Practice

Orthopedic Safety:

   traction

   casts

   appliances: brace, splints

   crutches

   never adjusting or tampering with equipment

Proper use of the following:

   strollers

   walkers

   wheelchairs

   stretchers

   restraints

   high chairs

   playpens

   transporting children

   lifting and bending

   equipment storage

Feeding

   name band identification of children

   dietary restrictions

   NPO (includes chewing gum/toothbrushing)

   how to hold baby for bottle feeding

   never propping baby's bottle

   proper positioning of infants after feeding

Orientation and Training Resources

	Dates Completed	
	Discussion	**Practice**
meal tray policies: serving/removing		
snack policies		
never offering food/drink without consent of staff		
diabetic precautions		
special protocols, such as those for eating disorders		

Infection Control/Isolation Precautions

do not come if you are sick or contagious		
keep your health record current		
categories of isolation and specific precautions		
use of gloves, gowns, masks		
disposal of linens, gowns, masks		
diapering, saving diapers, waste disposal		
universal precautions		
toy cleaning/disinfecting		
handwashing — why, when, how		
reading instructions before entering isolation rooms		

Medical Equipment

IV/central line functions/precautions		
oxygen precautions		
reasons for special positioning of children		
never reposition child without staff consent		

Management, Selection, Training & Supervision

Appendix B

	Dates Completed	
	Discussion	Practice

Emergencies

    accidents: what to do, how to report

    fire: reporting procedures, exiting

    disaster

    medical emergency

    seizure

    fall

    IV

    other emergencies:

    reporting unusual visitors

Toy Selection Safety

    age appropriate materials

    no parts which can be swallowed/inhaled

    no sharp corners or breakable toys

    only new stuffed toys

    isolation toys/policies

Toy Sorting/Cleaning Policy/Procedure

    wash toys mouthed by infants

Orientation and Training Resources

	Dates Completed	
	Discussion	Practice

Playroom Safety
- never leave child unattended
- position self to watch all children
- careful placement of all cords
- no smoking
- no friction toys near oxygen
- electrical outlets
- all cleaning materials out of reach
- toy/equipment storage
- limits/limit setting

Other areas where play is allowed:

_____

Outdoor/playground safety:
- equipment
- policies

List of things I wish to review or practice further:

_____
_____
_____
_____

Checklist reviewed with supervisor: _____
                                              Signature

Source: Arlene Kiely, Training Consultant, ACCH, Bethesda, MD

Appendix B

Confidentiality: A Volunteer's Obligations

I, _____, have requested to be a volunteer at _____.
I understand that as a volunteer I may have access to confidential patient information or confidential information about the family of the patient.

I understand that any information that I learn about a patient is confidential and that information about a patient can not be disclosed to anyone. I understand that law provides for possible civil and criminal penalties for disclosure of confidential patient information.

I agree that I will not:

- Reveal to anyone the name or identity of a patient.
- Repeat to anyone any statements or communications made by or about the patient.
- Reveal to anyone any information that I learn about the patient as a result of discussions with others providing care to the patient.
- Write or publish any articles, papers, stories or other written materials which will contain the names of any patient or information from which the names or identities of any patient can be discerned. If a paper is written about my volunteer work here, I agree that I will submit it to the director for approval.

I have read this statement. I understand my obligation to maintain patient confidentiality and I agree to follow that obligation.

Signed_____

Print Name_____

Address_____

Telephone_____

Witness_____

Adapted from: The University of Chicago Hospitals, Child Life and Family Education, Chicago, Illinois.

Confidentiality And Privacy Exercise

Confidentiality Exercise

Every child and family has a legal right to expect that we will keep all information private. What exactly must we do to make sure confidentiality is preserved? How many specific actions can you list?

_____
_____
_____
_____
_____
_____

It may help to imagine yourself or someone else close to you receiving health services here. What are the ways you would expect confidentiality to be preserved?

_____
_____
_____
_____
_____
_____

Privacy Exercise (Group or Individual)

Privacy is also essential in health care settings. What privacy would you expect if you were receiving care or services here? What actions must staff and volunteers take to respect child and family privacy?

_____
_____
_____
_____
_____

Source: Arlene Kiely, Training Consultant, ACCH, Bethesda, MD

Appendix B

Confidentiality and Privacy

What Volunteers Need to Know

CHILDREN AND FAMILIES have a legal right to expect that confidentiality of information will be preserved. Unlawful use or disclosure of information may expose an agency to civil and criminal liability. **Any breach of confidentiality must result in the automatic dismissal of a volunteer.**

Confidentiality means that all information about a child and family is protected.

- Protected information includes any and all information about a child and family, including, name, diagnosis, address, financial information, family relationships, and any information learned from the staff, child, or family.

- No photographs or videotapes of any kind are permissible without a signed photo release from the parents or guardians. Volunteers must not allow anyone to photograph or videotape without staff permission and a signed photo consent.

- Volunteers do not discuss the child, diagnosis, condition, treatment, or family information with anyone other than appropriate agency personnel. "What you hear and see here, stays here."

- Volunteers will discuss information only in private spaces and *not* in elevators, hallways, cafeteria, lobbies, waiting rooms, parking lot, or other public space in the agency or elsewhere. Volunteers must observe these precautions even if others occasionally forget them.

- Only authorized students may keep journals or written reports. All such written materials must first have format and content approved by the designated staff supervisor. Names and information that could identify a specific child or family may not be used under any circumstances.

- All issues of concern will be shared only with the appropriate staff.

- Volunteers may not have access to patient's charts.

Privacy involves privacy of body, belongings, information and space. It means that:

- A child and family can expect staff and volunteers to assure adequate clothing and covering to protect individual modesty. (Children younger than three years of age generally have not developed a sense of physical modesty.)

- Beyond age four, children need bathroom privacy and curtains drawn for use of urinals, bedpans, and bed baths.
- Volunteers never proceed past a drawn curtain without asking permission from the child or family being shielded.
- Knock on doors and get permission before entering. (This courtesy is frequently violated in institutions.)
- When a telephone call comes for a child or parent, offer to leave the room. Do not give out any information over the telephone, but refer such requests to the appropriate staff person or family member.
- Whenever possible private visiting spaces should be provided and respected.
- A place to store personal belongings should be provided and respected.
- Volunteers respect the privacy of mail and personal belongings of children and families.

Source: Arlene Kiely, Training Consultant, ACCH, Bethesda, MD

Appendix B

Infection Control

What Volunteers Need to Know

WHAT DO VOLUNTEERS need to know to prevent the spread of infection? Let's talk about germs without using medical jargon.

Remember:

- Well people may be carrying germs that could affect people who are sick.
- People who are sick are more susceptible to added infection.
- Some people who are sick may already have, or be coming down with, a contagious illness.

Therefore, our job is to do everything possible to prevent the spread of germs between children, families, staff, volunteers, visitors — in short, everyone here.

What does this mean?

- First, keep yourself well. Make sure the required medical records, TB test, doctor's statement, and immunization record are on file with your volunteer record. *Do not* come to volunteer if you are sick, have a cold, diarrhea, vomiting, rash, or any contagious condition. (Some agencies add, if anyone in your family has anything contagious.) Wear clean washable clothing. Protect your clothing with the agency smock or jacket.

- Did you know that handwashing with soap and water is *the most effective protection* against infection? Wash your hands before and after every patient contact, before and after handling any food, after using restrooms, after changing diapers or handling any body fluids, and before and after feeding a child.

- Learn and practice the agency's isolation techniques. They are designed to prevent the spread of infection. You don't need a medical degree to understand isolation rules. A clinic or emergency room will have a procedure for isolating individuals who may be contagious. Residential facilities, such as hospitals, will have specific categories of isolation.

Since procedures may vary slightly within agencies, we will not attempt a step-by-step procedure here. Read and learn the isolation rules of your agency. Ask your supervisor for them, and for a review checklist to verify your knowledge. The safety checklist also indicates many important things you will need to learn about infection control.

However, one way to make sense out of isolation rules is: to know how particular germs enter the body. All isolation rules are based on keeping germs from entering the body. When you know where a particular germ is likely to enter and also where it attacks the body, you understand what precautions must be followed to prevent this from happening.

Germs are present in the air you breathe, in feces, in blood, and in other body fluids such as saliva and semen. Germs can enter the body through the nose, the mouth, breaks in the skin (through wounds or needles), and through sexual intercourse. Anytime you come in contact with contaminated material you run the risk of infection if you are not using appropriate precautions and fail to wash your hands thoroughly afterward.

Respiratory Precaution

FOR EXAMPLE, certain germs, such as a virus which causes the common cold, are airborne. How does air enter the body? Through breathing. Respiratory Precautions is the term usually used to describe precautions against airborne germs, since these enter by and also attack the respiratory system. Therefore, wearing a mask over the nose and mouth keeps out airborne germs. Covering the nose and mouth with a tissue when coughing or sneezing prevents airborne droplets from being inhaled by others. Handwashing before and after working with a child is essential, since saliva from a child could remain on the hands.

Wound and Skin Precautions

NORMALLY, THE SKIN protects the body from germs. However, some germs enter through breaks in the skin, and cause infection, redness, soreness, and pus. Until a skin break, such as a surgical incision, has healed a person is susceptible to infection from the outside. Sterile dressings help protect wounds while they are healing. Germs *from* an infected wound can also be spread to others, not through the air, but through direct contact with pus or fluid from the wound. Therefore, sterile gloves are worn by staff when changing dressings. Strict handwashing before or after any contact with the wound or soiled dressings is the rule. While volunteers don't change dressings, they may come in contact with or notice soiled dressings. Therefore, volunteers observe handwashing at all times, and report any soiled dressings to staff for attention. For close contact, such as rocking a baby, volunteers should wear a gown when working with children who need wound and skin precautions.

Enteric Precautions

SOME GERMS ENTER through the mouth, and can be present in the stomach and its contents, (such as vomit), or in the intestines and feces in the body's digestive, or enteric (intestinal) system. Therefore, enteric precautions are used in these situations. This means protecting by wearing a gown, and using gloves (if changing soiled diapers, or emptying bed pans), or having contact with saliva, (such as when feeding young children), or any vomited materials. Again, strict thorough handwashing before and after working with a child is essential.

Most agencies post isolation rules on the door of the patients' rooms. This serves to remind everyone of the particular precautions that are needed.

- Reading the rules is not enough!
- Ask for a demonstration of each isolation technique, particularly for the proper way to put on and take off gowns, masks, and gloves. Ask a staff person to demonstrate and then observe your practice of each technique, including the proper *disposal* of gowns, masks, and gloves.
- Contaminated materials are disposed of separately from all other trash. Specially marked sealed bags, safety containers, and other means are essential protection.
- When in doubt, ask! Review the posted precautions, no matter how well you understand them. Health and safety depends on it.

A Word About AIDS

WHAT ABOUT HIV INFECTION? Have isolation precautions changed because of it? The answer is yes, and no. Sometimes, *YES*. Because it is not always possible to know whether or not a contagious disease exists, all health care agencies require staff to use **UNIVERSAL PRECAUTIONS** anytime they are likely to come in contact with blood or body fluids. This is especially true in emergency situations where a person's disease status is uncertain. Universal precautions are to protect the skin and mucous membranes, and include:

- wearing a gown if you are likely to be in contact with body fluids or mucous membranes;
- wearing gloves when likely to touch body substances or mucous membranes;
- wearing a mask and eye cover if any splashing into mouth or eyes is likely; and
- using extreme caution when handling needles, scalpels, sharp instruments, and disposing of them in safety containers.

Why, then, do we say that usual precautions have not changed? *Since most routine activities of daily living (such as eating and playing) do not involve contact with blood or body fluids, normal daily care does not require isolation precautions.* This is because the human immunodeficiency virus is very fragile and cannot survive outside the human body. It must have an environment of blood or body fluids to survive. The virus can't live in air. It can't survive on objects, such as plates or pillows. This means you can't breathe it in through the air. You can't catch it just by touching objects used by a person with HIV infection. You can't catch it just by being in the same room or touching a person with HIV infection. (However, thorough handwashing and protection from skin breaks should be observed, as always.)

Touching, hugging, rocking, cradling, snuggling, and all the warm nurturing activities that express affection and promote a sense of well being are especially needed by people with HIV infection. Volunteers, because they are usually not qualified or expected to engage in medical procedures, are ideally suited to provide acceptance and reassurance by engaging in normal daily activities and supportive relationships with these children and their families.

Health care needs are changing constantly. HIV infection is only one example of the need for caring, qualified individuals who will gain the knowledge, skill, and commitment needed by new challenges for service. Because there are increasing numbers of children with HIV infection, many volunteers will be needed to support these children and families. Understanding normal precautions is important. Understanding human needs for a normal environment and normal contact is equally important.

Source: Arlene Kiely, Training Consultant, ACCH, Bethesda, MD

Appendix B

The Psychological Impact of Illness And Hospitalization Upon The Child — Infancy to Twelve Years

THOSE OF US WHO have spent many years working in hospitals have come to take much for granted. We know we are kind, benevolent, capable people interested in healing, the alleviation of suffering and the prolongation of life. However, a child coming into a hospital for the first time may see us quite differently. No matter how well we do our job, we are not his parents, the hospital bed is not his own and the world we provide is an unfamiliar and frightening one. It is a world in which children are hurt. Every body orifice may be entered and when these are exhausted we create new openings by injection, I.V., cut-down or surgery.

To understand the child's feelings about hospitalization, we must first understand the child's view of his world and those concerns which normally accompany his particular stage of development. He fears separation from his parents, bodily injury, needles, disfigurement, helplessness and death. Unfortunately, the experience of illness and hospitalization is likely to confirm the validity of all these fears.

In her book, *Children in the Hospital* (1), Thesi Bergman says, "With the physically healthy child, the fears of castration, death and annihilation are products of his fantasy, recognized as such by his maturing reason.... Since they have no place in external reality, they dissolve when they become conscious and are understood.... However, with seriously ill or damaged children, fantasy and reality coincide, the latter leading back to the former. Castration appears more feasible where limbs are actually attacked by illness and rendered useless.... Even complete annihilation cannot seem impossible after the devastating experience of having one's whole life altered or shattered by catching an infection or by having an accident. It is probably this addition of the terrifying reality to the usual frightening fantasy life of childhood which tips the scales for some children and presents them with the task which they cannot and do not want to solve." (p. 106)

In addition to those concerns appropriate to the child's developmental age, we must also consider the experience which he may have had with sickness and death. Perhaps a sibling died of the same disease which the child has, or an apparently healthy grandmother went to the hospital only to die. Perhaps he feels that people only come to hospitals to have babies.

The Young Infant (Birth to Six Months)

IN HOSPITALIZING THE CHILD under six months of age, we must realize that an extended hospitalization may cause the child to be deprived of appropriate stimulation and relationship experience. In fact, if I wanted, for some diabolical reason, to design a depriving environment for a child, I would create a neat, clean institution in which he was separated from his parents and was cared for by a great many people each day. I would make sure that the people worked in shifts and that from day to day on each shift the child was cared for by a different person. I would also create a setting in which specific attention was paid to the child's physical needs, including his temperature, respiration, digestion and elimination, to the exclusion of any recognition of his emotional and relationship needs. I would specify that he be kept in his bed as much as possible and certainly never be let out of his room, the door to which would always be closed.

We are often guilty of creating such a depriving situation for the premature baby, who must spend the first weeks of life in a hospital, much of that time in an incubator. He needs the life support systems it provides, but not the isolation from human contact is creates.

We may also deprive the child with a congenital physical condition who requires hospitalization for several months immediately after birth or the child who develops a serious illness or physical condition necessitating prolonged hospitalization in the first three years of life.

The Older Infant and Toddler (Six Months to Two Years)

WITHOUT EXCEPTION, research has indicated that it is the older infant and toddler who is most vulnerable to the effects of hospitalization.

As Robertson (8) states, "If going to the hospital means leaving the care of his mother, as it usually does, this is inevitably an intensely unhappy experience for the small child, no matter how kindly he is cared for by the doctors and nurses. An older child, a child of eight or ten years, for instance, can understand why he is in a hospital and cooperate in treatment and make friends all around the ward, and if treated with the kindness that he will usually meet, he can be made reasonably content although away from his family. But the child of under three or four is quite different because of his intense and almost exclusive attachment to his mother, which is normal in the first years of life. If in this phase of development, the young child loses his mother's care on going into the hospital, he will react with acute and persisting stress. He is too young to understand the necessity for the separation and at this age there is no way of preparing him for it. All he knows is that the person in whom his expectations of comfort and security are vested is not there to meet his urgent need of her. He is instantly plugged into grief and despair." (p.13)

David Levy (5) has divided the young child's adjustment to hospitalization into three periods: protest, despair, and denial. The period of protest may last from a few hours to several days during which time the child is grief-stricken, cries loudly, shakes his crib, throws himself about and may reject the nurses. The period of despair is characterized by intense need of his mother, combined with a hopeless feeling that he will never see her again. During this period the child may withdraw from ward personnel.

In the stage of denial, the child may superficially show more interest in his surroundings, and may even appear happy. This is often taken as an encouraging sign by the staff, yet actually it indicates that the child is resigning himself to the situation and is suppressing his feelings of grief and fear. Unfortunately, at this point, the staff may feel that the child has finally "settled in" and has forgotten his mother. At one time it was a common practice in pediatric hospitals to forbid the parents to visit for a month to encourage this process of "settling in".

Levy (5) feels that the negative reactions in children of this age (infancy to two years) are so severe (are in fact like combat neuroses) that wherever possible it is best to postpone any elective surgery until he has the comprehension and ability to master his anxiety.

The Preschool Child (Two to Five Years)

CONCERNS ABOUT SEPARATION from the mother continue to predominate in the preschool child. Additionally, he is developing many concerns about body injury and mutilation. His understanding of anatomy is at best inexact and at worst severely distorted. On various occasions, young children have told me in all sincerity that the tonsils are located in the groin and in the center of the brain!

When a preschool child goes for surgery, he may fear that in some poorly defined way he will emerge a different person or that the surgeon will not confine himself to the indicative operative field. One little boy was terrified that the surgeon would remove his belly button while ostensibly operating on him for a hernia. Another child, in for a T. and A. was afraid she would wake up blind. This fantasy was encouraged by a well-meaning nurse who, just before the child was anesthetized, said, "You have such pretty eyes, I think that while you are asleep, I will ask the doctor to exchange them for mine."

Preschool, as well as school age children, commonly feel that they are sick as a punishment for their own badness. I was told by a post-polio patient that boys get polio "because they go into the woods when their mother tells them not to," and I was told by a little girl who was a congenital amputee, that "Little girls lose their arms because their mothers get mad at them for being bad."

In a study by Beverly (2), 90 percent of cardiac and diabetic children when asked why children get sick, answered, "Because they are bad." Asked why they had heart disease they said, "Because I ran too much," on being asked, "Why did you get diabetes?", they replied, "Because I ate too much sugar."

Bergman (1) reports a case of a little boy who felt that children became ill because they picked up germs in the course of masturbation. To invalidate this theory, he told another child that when one got sick from touching one's penis, it was cured with "Penicillin".

The School Age Child
(Five to Twelve Years)

WITH EVERY YOUNG SCHOOL AGE CHILD (ages five to seven) the primary concerns are about hospitalization and separation, but they are also fears about needles and about being operated on. As the child grows older and approaches adolescence, concern about the hospitalization and separation will lessen, but there will be increasing concern about the operative procedure and about the experience of being anesthetized. Not only is he afraid that he will suffocate, but he is distressed by the loss of control and feeling of helplessness which accompanies the experience of being anesthetized. In fact, one of his greatest concerns about the hospitalization itself will relate to the infantalizing aspects of hospitalization. As Bergman (1) says:

> Adult patients who, while being healthy, feel certain of their independence in body matters, can during physical illness permit themselves to return temporarily to the state of a helpless infant whose body is under other people's care and jurisdiction. It is impossible for children to accept nursing in the same spirit. For them, to have obtained a measure of physical independence from the adult world and to have personal control over their own bodies are great developmental achievements which they prize highly and are reluctant to renounce. They may show this by obstructive and uncooperative behavior as a defense against the regressive move which the situation demands from them; or they may feel unable to keep up their more mature status and slip back entirely into passive compliance, allowing themselves to be handled without resistance. Both reactions are unwelcome and unhelpful from the practical point of view of dealing with the ill body as well as from the aspect of smooth, progressive mental development. (p. 143)

The Outcome of the Hospital Experience

IN JUSTIFYING THEIR LACK OF ATTENTION to the child's emotional needs and his understanding of his hospitalization, many hospital personnel have taken the view that "the child will get over it." There are indications that to a certain extent, particularly with older children, this is true. However, even those older children may have undergone a period of unnecessary terror and suffering before "getting over it." Additionally, there is abundant research evidence that there is a large group of children, particularly younger ones, who suffer significant, long term distortions in development as a direct result of hospitalization.

It is important that medical personnel remember two basic tenets of medical ethics: that the physician "do no harm" and that he alleviate suffering. Certainly the physician should feel compelled to do no harm to a child emotionally and to alleviate emotional suffering as well as physical.

To briefly summarize some of the literature on the sequelae of hospitalization in children, James Robertson (8) reports on 246 hospitalizations of children under five years of age. In more than 100 of these cases, there were significant emotional upsets in the children upon returning home. Forty of these cases showed severe and/or prolonged and continuing distress over months or years. The reactions included rage at the parents, long term loss of trust, sleep and eating disturbances, regression in development, (particularly in terms of self-help activities, such as toilet training and feeding) violent temper tantrums, fear of strangers, and continuing fear of anyone in a white uniform.

Similarly, Prugh (7) reports on a study of 100 children who were hospitalized for an average of 8 days. Fifty of these children were in an experimental program which included daily visiting by parents, early ambulation, a play program, and psychological preparation for surgery. The fifty children in the control group were in a traditional ward arrangement in which parents were permitted to visit once a week for two hours, children were not given the play program and were not prepared for procedures.

Thirty-eight percent of the two to twelve year olds in the control group showed severe reactions (defined as a significant anxiety about hospitalization three months after discharge). Two-thirds of those showing severe reactions were in the two to five age group. With good ward management, the incidence of severe disturbance was halved in the experimental group, but still remained high.

WHILE THE INVESTIGATORS found that the sex of the child or the severity of the illness was not related to the degree of disturbance, the children who were considered to be at highest risk for disturbance were those under four years of age, those with the least satisfactory relationship with the parents, those who had undergone severe stress in the hospital and those who had obvious problems in adaptation in the hospital.

Prugh (7) concluded that for most children under four years of age, no amount of love and understanding would make up for the absence of the mother.

In a study of Blom (3) of 143 children aged 2 to 14 who underwent T. and A. at Massachusetts General Hospital, he found that 25 of these children showed a transient disturbance lasting 10 days or less. He also found negative reactions to be far more common in the child under five.

Anyone wishing to have a comprehensive review of the literature on the emotional effect of illness and hospitalization and the child should refer to Mason's (6) article.

Having considered the negative outcomes of badly managed hospital experience, it is important to realize that there may be positive outcomes of such an experience. First of all, the child may develop new coping techniques and a better understanding of his world. Solnit (10) reports that even in very young children, hospitalization can be used to overcome certain developmental obstacles.

Ideally, a well handled hospitalization will lead to a new sense of trust on the part of the child and a more positive view of doctors and hospitals. It may also be seen by the child as a step towards maturity, an initiation rite to growing up.

Parental Involvement

IF WE ARE TO BRING about a positive outcome and avoid the more negative ones which I have described, changes must be made in traditional hospital procedure. First of all, parents (particularly mothers) must obviously be included in plans for the child's hospitalization. Mothers should not only be permitted to room in with their children, but should be actively encouraged to do so. When a toddler is to be hospitalized and family obligations prevent the mother from rooming in, she should be provided with homemaker services at home to permit her to stay with the child.

In addition to rooming in, we must have more liberal visiting hours than are permitted in many hospitals. Not many years ago at Children's Hospital in Washington, D.C., we had only two visiting hours per week, one hour on Sunday afternoon and one hour on Wednesday afternoon. As the appointed hour approached, the anxious parents milled about in the waiting room waiting for the signal that the time had come and they would begin the rush to the elevators. The ward was then inundated with parents who left a group of screaming children in their wake. Parents felt compelled to remain with their child for one hour, no matter what, and clung desperately to him in anticipation of the several days that would follow before they could be together again. Nurses were overwhelmed with demands from parents. The introduction of almost unlimited visiting hours virtually eliminated these problems.

In addition to being allowed to stay with their children, parents need to be prepared for the experience of their child's hospitalization. Frequently parents avoid preparing the child because they themselves do not have a clear understanding of what will happen, or do not appreciate the need for preparation.

Additionally, parents should be allowed to participate in the care of their child. While treatment and administration of medication should be left to the medical staff, there is no reason that mothers cannot continue to bathe, dress, toilet and comfort their children while they are in the hospital.

Basically, it is important that the hospital staff appreciate the validity of the parents' concerns and questions. It is a frightening thing to have a child snatched from you and placed in a situation totally beyond your control, no matter how kind the people who do it are. Frequently, the medical staff will react to a parent's anxiety as a personal insult, assuming that in expressing concern, the parent is questioning the staff's competency.

I also have seen staff members who regard the mother as a "natural enemy" who will inevitably interfere with the treatment. Consciously or unconsciously, they are in competition with the mother to prove that they can be a better mother than she. I have always felt that the common practice in hospitals of referring to all mothers as "mother" rather than as "Mrs. Smith" or "Mrs. Jones" indicates an unconscious contempt for the mother and a refusal to recognize her legitimate status in the hospital.

Preparation for the Child

I WOULD HOPE THAT by this time there is no need for me to justify the need for emotional preparation of the child for painful or intrusive procedures or surgery. I therefore would like to discuss some general considerations in carrying out such preparation.

First of all, do not assume that because the child does not ask questions or verbally express fears, he does not have questions or fears. The child is quick to sense when the adults taking care of him do not want to answer questions and therefore may avoid asking them. Also, his fears and his conceptions are often so horrendous that he is reluctant to make them more real by putting them into words. He may be embarrassed to admit to his fears, feeling that surely he is the only person in the world who has ever had these concerns.

Sometimes, as a defense against his own anxiety, a child will paint a very rosy picture and be quite jovial about coming to the hospital. I remember a patient of mine, an eight year old boy, who was scheduled for open heart surgery. As he left the house with his parents to come to the hospital, he said, "I can't wait until I get to Children's Hospital. I'll have such fun. I'll be able to see Dr. Robinson every day. I know everyone will give me presents." At that point his father wisely said, "If you want to cry, its really all right." The child immediately burst into tears.

Additionally, the child's fears may be expressed indirectly or symbolically, rather than in direct, obvious ways. I will never forget the little boy who, immediately before a herniorrhaphy, sat counting his fingers "to see if they were all there." I am pretty sure that it was not one of his fingers that he was afraid would be amputated!

In preparing children, you must be honest. This does not mean that you must include every gory detail of the operation, but you must tell the child in simple terms, what is going to happen to him, how he will look when he wakes up, how he will feel and why the procedure is being done. Certainly do not tell him that it will not hurt him when it will.

Please do not ask "for a stiff upper lip" or tell him "big boys (or girls) don't cry." With such remarks you are not only making the child feel guilty about honest feelings, but denying him an important outlet to those feelings. Certainly do not point out to him that there are a lot of children worse off than he is, and that he therefore should not complain. Taken to its most ridiculous extent, this sort of reasoning can even be applied to the dying patient, for we can always tell him that someone down the hall is dying a more terrible death than his and he shouldn't complain!

When you are preparing a child, first determine what his conceptions and misconceptions are about what is to be done to him. Frequently if you present him immediately with the facts, you may not give him an opportunity to work out his particular fantasies about the procedure. Also do not be discouraged if these fantasies persist, along with the factual information.

For what should you prepare the child? First of all, particularly with a verbal child, you simply prepare him for the appearance of the hospital. Those of us who have worked in hospitals for many years fail to realize that they are really strange looking places full of frightening equipment and men in green suits and masks.

Secondly, it is wise to prepare a child for the most basic sort of hospital routine. Tell him that on admission he will be weighed, measured, his temperature taken and that he will be given a hospital gown and a bed of his own.

Prepare the child for being anesthetized if he is going into surgery. Without getting too technical, you can tell him that he will smell funny smelling gas that will make him sleepy and dizzy. Emphasize that it will put him to sleep sufficiently so that he will not have any pain during surgery, but please emphasize that he will wake up!

IN ANTICIPATION OF A SURGICAL PROCEDURE, tell the child why he is going to have the procedure, including roughly what the surgeons will be doing. It is remarkably reassuring to know that surgeons have small, precise instruments with which to snip out tonsils rather than large pliers with which to yank them out! Do not have the idea that the child does not care what we do to him while he is asleep, for you can be sure that he does care.

Prepare the child for his awakening in the recovery room. Many surgeons feel that children have no memory of the recovery room, and for some this may be true, but as long as we require some degree of consciousness before the child is released, then there is a good chance that he will remember it. He should know that the recovery room is a rather strange looking place in which he will meet nurses that he has not met before and that his mother will not be there. However, he should be assured that as soon as he can talk to the nurse, he will be returned to his mother. Tell him that the recovery room has bright lights and that the beds are tilted. Prepare him for the fact that he will see some rather strange equipment which is there to help children who need help, but that he may not need any of the equipment.

Prepare the child for how he will feel afterwards, letting him know that he may feel nauseated or in pain and assuring him that something will be done about the pain. Also let him know how he will look after the surgery if he must have drainage tubes, what kind of bandages he will have and what his incision will be like.

If it is probable that the child will go to intensive care from the operating room, he should be prepared for this experience. I saw this done beautifully by the nurses in the intensive care unit at Children's Hospital in D.C. The patient was a boy of eight who was to have open heart surgery. They showed him the bed they hoped would be his, although they told him there was a chance that another child might need that particular bed. They took him about the room and demonstrated all the equipment, including the respirator, which they indicated was a friend that would be available to him if he needed help breathing. They also quite ingeniously pointed to the wall clock which was hanging askew and told him that when he saw that funny clock he would know that he was among friends. His first words in the intensive care were, "There's the funny clock."

Obviously, children should be prepared for even minor procedures. As Bergman (1) says, "What blocks understanding here is the normal adult's unfamiliarity with the child's subjective, irrational, emotional approach. Adult understanding comes more readily where psychic reality and external reality coincide and the child's fears are concerned with unquestionably serious situations which cannot fail to evoke anybody's concern and sympathy ... However, it is easy to establish the fact that, so far as fantasies, anxieties, and affects are concerned, the piercing of a boil, the taking of a blood sample, or the extraction of a tooth may loom as large to the child, as the actual removal of an eye or the amputation of a limb. What needs to be understood is the fact that in both instances, whether objectively justified or not, the patient's emotions are very real and the child is in need of help." (p. 137)

Another aspect of preparation of the child is the techniques which are to be employed. With older school age children this can be done through a rather straightforward discussion. With children of all ages, use may be made of puppets, or playroom interviews, of models of equipment and facilities, of drawings (made not only by the hospital staff, but by the child to reveal his misunderstanding of anatomy), of tours of facilities, (such as I described with the boy in intensive care) and of explanation of equipment such as respirators, suction pumps, oxygen tents and intravenous solutions. It is also extremely reassuring to the child to meet with another patient who has had the same surgery. He is living proof that children do survive having their tonsils out!

Emergency admissions bring their own problems, but certainly, even here, as long as the child is conscious and unless he is in extremis, a brief and simple explanation of what has happened to him and what you are going to do can be made.

Need for Change in Hospital Organization

SOME OF THE SUGGESTIONS which I have made are obviously going to necessitate changes in the way in which hospitals are organized. Frequently, they are going to necessitate a choice between efficiency and the meeting of human needs. It is perhaps more efficient to assign nurses to particular duties rather than to individual patients, but in terms of human needs, it is far more preferable for a child to have his own particular nurse who is responsible for all aspects of his care.

Additionally, I would suggest that a child be allowed to wear his own street clothes whenever this is realistically possible. Our need to pop people into bed and put them into hospital clothes the minute they hit the ward makes me wonder if we think that without hospital garb we might not be able to tell the patients from the staff and some might escape.

Let the child be out of his bed as much as possible. Sometimes the necessity to keep a child in bed is dictated by his medical condition, more often it is dictated by a lack of space in the particular hospital facility, and this is something that should be considered in the design of hospitals. If early ambulation is desirable, the patient has to have some place to ambulate!

Please do not discuss the child at his bedside. As Vanderveer (11) said more than 23 years ago "Pernicious is the bedside discussion conducted about the child and within his hearing, though without his participation, in a language full of strange words and reference to stranger diagnostic techniques. This hoary rite which is still practiced almost universally, may arouse great fear in the patient about what is wrong with him or what is being done to him." (p. 60). Also, do not discuss one child's condition in from of another child, because no matter what, he will be convinced that you are talking about him.

If you put up a sign relating to the child (Nothing by mouth, Noting Prep) explain to him why it is there. If he is old enough to read he is going to wiggle around in his bed until he can read it (and perhaps not understand it) and if he is not old enough to read it he will still know that it relates to himself and he will be certain that it says something quite frightening like, "This is a bad boy who is to be punished."

We must also do whatever we can, and perhaps this is a job of hospital architects, to change the institutional and medical appearance of hospitals. We seem to have gone from antiseptic white to operating room green. Since a recent ad for surgeon's gloves indicated that they were available in "six glorious colors" there certainly must be something we could do about the appearance of hospital beds, corridors and rooms.

Need for Change in Point of View of Staff

MY FOLLOWING REMARKS are probably going to be the most controversial of all, for I am going to suggest that if we are to meet the emotional needs of hospitalized children, we must change some of our time-honored ideas. First, we are going to have to decide that it does not take too much time to prepare a child for surgery or intrusive procedures, or to answer his general questions. As Bergman (1) says "The point is frequently made that it would add to the heavy burden carried by the hospital staff if emotional implications were taken seriously by them, alongside the physical ones with which they are concerned. Whether this would in fact be the case is still an open question. As matters stand at present, no greater gulf can be imagined than that existing between the practical factual and realistic approach of most medical and nursing personnel in the pediatric wards and the unrealistic, affective response of their patients — a gulf which in many instances precludes cooperation and the building up of positive relationships, and causes as much exasperation on the one side as it causes distress and unhappiness on the other." (p. 145)

We must re-examine the idea that "the child will get over it" (the emotional effects of hospitalization) and/or that he will "forget this in a couple of days." While it is true that many children will "get over it" in that they will not commit suicide, go to jail, or be committed to a mental hospital, a large percentage of children, particularly young children and their parents, will have endured a significant period of suffering.

Another idea that I would like to banish forever is that it is not good to worry a child in advance of surgery by preparing him for it. This is fallacious for several reasons. First, at some point, the child is going to have to find out what you have done to him, and when he awakens confused and in pain is not the ideal time for him to make the discovery.

Second, any child who has been lured into a hospital and not told what will happen, will experience a tremendous and perhaps, permanent loss of trust in his parents and in doctors when he finds that they have deceived him.

Third, the child will have been deprived of the function of "anticipatory anxiety." There is a great deal of research to indicate that when an individual has time to anticipate an upsetting event, he is able to marshall his defenses and better able to master the event.

FINALLY, AN UNPREPARED and terrified child is a more difficult one to treat and the somatic concommitants of his terror may actually interfere with the process of recovery.

I would also like to dispel the idea that "parents only make trouble and upset the child." It is only with their parents that children are free to show their grief and distress and the "settling in" of the child who has not been visited by his parents is not true forgetfulness but despair.

Certainly there are difficult parents, but they are often difficult because of their concerns about their child. All too often we encounter the pesky or withdrawn parent. We find that such parents are usually incapable of providing adequate support and security for their child and frequently have an adverse effect on his reaction to hospitalization. It is also our experience that such parental behavior is often motivated by feelings of anxiety, guilt, fear or ignorance. Frequently the withdrawn parent may simply not know that she can be involved with the child's care, or may not feel welcome in the strangeness of the hospital environment. It is our responsibility to reach out to such parents and include them in the planning of their child's care. In the nursing units this is accomplished in various ways. Often, it is through simple courtesies such as introducing the members of the treatment team, or providing parents with information concerning the cafeteria hours. It may involve orienting them to the physical layout of the of the unit, or expressing an interest in the child's home environment and his siblings. Often more complex intervention is required such as assisting parents in explaining the treatment plan to the child. Many parents need help in leaving their child and must be alerted to the danger of "sneaking away." The supportive role of the nurse may also include assisting parents to plan for the child's home care or helping them to adjust to a terminal illness.

It may involve organizing groups of parents so that common problems and feelings can be shared. In all cases, it is our goal and commitment in pediatric nursing to help parents feel more capable in their role rather than guilty and insecure in the hospital environment." (pg. 92)

Finally, I would like to lay to rest that hoary maxim that "the hospital staff must never become emotionally involved with patients." You must never forget that you are simply human beings, albeit highly trained ones, trying to meet the needs of other human beings who are desperately in need of your care and understanding. There are many occasions when a smile, a comforting pat on the shoulder, or a hand to hold before going into surgery mean far more to the patient than any medication you could give. I foresee the day when the problems of diagnosis and prescription of treatment may largely be taken over by computers. However, there can never be any substitute for the honest, human concern of the medical staff. As a well-known British physician used to say, "The physician and the nurse must never forget that their most powerful medicine is themselves."

Source: Mary E. Robinson, Ph.D., Clinical Psychologist, Rockville, MD

Appendix B

List of References

1. Bergman, Thesi, Children in the Hospital, International Universities Press, New York, 1965
2. Beverly, Bert, The Effect of Illness upon Emotional Development, Journal of Pediatrics, 8, May, 1936, 533-600
3. Blom, Gasten, The Reactions of Hospitalized Children to Illness, Pediatrics, 22, September, 1958, 590-600
4. Jessner, Lucille, Blom G., and Waldfogel, S., Emotional Implications of Tonsillectomy and Adenoidectomy of Children, Psychoanalytic Study of the Child, 7, 1952, 126
5. Levy, David, Psychic Trauma of Operations in Children, American Journal of Diseases of Children, 69, 1945, 7-15
6. Mason, Edward, The Hospitalized Child — His Emotional Needs, New England Journal of Medicine, 272 February, 1954, 406-414
7. Prugh, Dean, A Study of Emotional Reactions of Children and Families to Hospitalization and Illness, American Journal of Orthopsychiatry, 23, 1953 70-106
8. Robertson, James, Hospitals and Children: A Parent's Eye View, International Universities Press, New York, 1962
9. Schwalenstocker, Anne, and Frevert, Elaine, Editorial Comment, Clinical Proceedings of the Children's Hospital National Medical Center, 28, 4, April 1972, 91-92
10. Solnit, Albert, Hospitalization — An Aid to Physical and Psychological Health in Childhood, Journal of Diseases of Children, 99, 1950, 155-163
11. Vanderveer, A.A., Psychopathology of Physical Illness and Hospital Residence, Quarterly Journal of Child Behavior, 1, January, 1949, 55-71

Family-Centered Care

MEDICAL CARE, EVEN IN THE MOST IDEAL SETTINGS, is a profound interruption in the life of a child and family. The best health care will be family centered, directed at preserving and strengthening family bonds. What is family-centered care? How can staff and volunteers make sure that their work with children also supports the family?

The philosophy of family-centered care begins by recognizing that the family is the constant in the child's life, while health care systems and personnel fluctuate over time. Family-centered caregivers believe that all families want what is best for their children, are deeply caring, and want to nurture and support their children. Thus, families must be respected as an essential part of the health care team. How can volunteers help?

Too often parents feel helpless, stripped of their normal role in a health care setting. They may react by seeming withdrawn and passive, overprotective, or even hostile. We do well to remember that few parents are at their best when their child's well-being seems to be at stake. In addition, the pressure of other responsibilities can demand both time and energy, taking parents away when they would like to be present. Many parents are reassured to know that trained volunteers can help give support to their children when they are unable to be present. Volunteers support, but do not supplant, the parental role. As one parent has stated, "By supporting the family, volunteers preserve what each child needs most, the best possible family."

Family-centered caregivers use many approaches to support the family. An important first step is recognizing that each family is unique and will have its own definition of who is considered family. In places where children stay overnight, families can be encouraged to supply photos of persons important to the child. Children may enjoy drawing a picture of their home or family.

Care that traditionally focussed on the needs of children now has expanded to center on the needs of family. This means that the family's right to make health care choices based on family needs is supported and respected. Assessment and planning that includes the family as essential and equal team members is considered the standard of excellence. Family-centered professionals and volunteers are committed to a free and open exchange of information in an honest and supportive manner.

Family-centered care recognizes that families will differ in the role they choose to adopt as part of the health care team and as part of their child's experience. Some families will choose to be actively involved in all care decisions, assuming the role of team leader. Others will choose a less active role depending on family needs. For example, one family may choose to have one parent present with a hospitalized child 24 hours a day. Another family may choose to visit before and after work, and have one parent

Appendix B

spend the night. Volunteers can support parents in their choices and help them to feel good about how they are able to care for their child. Family-centered professionals recognize and adapt to changing needs of the family over time.

What are some ways you can be helpful to families here? List your ideas, and discuss with your supervisor.

Source: Arlene Kiely, Training Consultant, ACCH, Bethesda, MD

Guidelines for Supporting Families

Suggestions appropriate in all settings:

- Be friendly and welcoming in greeting families. A calm manner can communicate caring and readiness to be of service.

- Be especially attentive to families who have come for the first time. Ask, "Can I help you?" . . . "Is there anything you need to know to be more comfortable here?"

- Avoid judging parents. Parents are probably not at their best when under stress. Volunteers will rarely have knowledge of all the possible stresses a parent faces, from worry and uncertainty about a child's health, competing responsibilities of work, home, and child care, financial strains. A parent worried about sick leave, bus fare, an unsympathetic boss, rent, and insurance may be too tired to notice a sick child's art work, or to deal well with a crying child.

- When parents seem particularly stressed, a volunteer can ask, "Is there anyone or anything I can get for you?" Also, letting the appropriate staff person know that the parent seems upset is important.

- Provide privacy time and space for parents and children to be together. You can leave graciously and say, "I'll be down the hall if you need anything. Is there anything you need before I go?"

- If you have toys or activities which you know are enjoyed at a certain age, or that a particular child enjoys, offer to get them or leave them for parent and child to enjoy together.

- Sometimes parents need a break, but feel they must remain with a child every minute. Volunteers can ask, "Let me know if you'd like me to play with your child while you take a break." Sometimes playing with the child while mom or dad reads or naps in the same room can be very supportive of parents.

- Parents may welcome opportunities to talk with volunteers, and may sometimes ventilate criticisms and fears. Listen but do not give advice. Encourage parents to seek appropriate staff for assistance.

- How can brothers and sisters be helped? Consider how to provide information and support in waiting areas, at home, following emergencies, or when families must be separated.

Further considerations in settings where children must remain overnight or longer:

- Be sensitive to children newly admitted, or admitted due to an emergency. There may not have been time for adequate preparation, or absorption, of information. Asking parents and children "Is there anything I can help you with?" does not mean having answers, but being willing to find out and refer to the appropriate staff person. In emergencies, people may easily forget what they have been told.

- Assume that all parents, including those who don't visit often, care about their children.

- Make parents feel welcome when they come. Avoid making them feel guilty. Parents need to know their child is well cared for when they are unable to be present.

- Assume that long-term children and families may still be unsure about certain information and may have gaps in their knowledge. It is easy to overlook them and miss needs. Special activities, programs and services may need frequent promotion.

- Encourage parents to let children know in advance when they must leave. Sneaking away is to be avoided as it can create anxiety and lack of trust. Tears can be accepted and supported. "Daddy will miss you, too, but he will come back when he can." Volunteers can offer to stay with child to ease leave-taking.

- Encourage parents not to make a promise they cannot keep. For example, don't promise a child "I'll be back tomorrow morning" if it is doubtful. It is better to say "I'll be back as soon as I can."

Source: Arlene Kiely, Training Consultant, ACCH, Bethesda, MD

Orientation and Training Resources

Reflections on Child Development

WHAT IS YOUR PERSONAL THEORY of child development? Everyone has a theory of child development, whether aware of it or not. These theories form the basis of our beliefs, attitudes and expectations about what is normal behavior for both children and parents. For example, each of the following quotes represents a very definite point of view about what is acceptable, expected, or normal:

- *"My children will never whine."*
- *"A good parent will never spank a kid."*
- *"Children should be seen and not heard."*
- *"Childhood should be happy and carefree."*
- *"Big boys don't cry."*
- *"Adults sometimes have to lie to children."*
- *"Children should always share."*
- *"A child should not be allowed to talk back to an adult."*

All these statements reflect strong opinions about relationships between adults and children, the role of adults, the kinds of behaviors expected of children and adults. Anyone who fully agrees with all of the above statements, is probably too opinionated to be able to effectively support children and their families in health care. The point is that most people have strong idea about childhood and parenting, based on personal experiences. It is important to be aware of, and examine one's most strongly held beliefs. They may, or may not be realistic. **Unexamined beliefs can stand in the way of being helpful to individual children and families.**

Fortunately, children thrive and survive a great variety of less than perfect parenting. Fatigue and other pressures can hinder the performance of even the most well-intentioned parents. All parents have said and done things they regret. Even the best volunteers and staff persons can expect to have an occasional bad day. Fortunately, children are resilient.

There are at least four guidelines volunteers need to remember to work effectively with children in health care settings:

1. Know what development is considered normal and therefore might be expected of children at a given age. You don't have to guess. Lists and readings will be provided. When an adult expects something which is not realistic for a child's age, frustration and problem occur.

2. Remember that illness and stress can cause children (and adults!) to regress.

3. Respect individual differences in temperament, and in coping and learning styles. Children aren't born as blank slates, but have certain inborn characteristics, or preferred modes of operations.

4. When adults are consistent in their behavior, children know what to expect and are more secure. A good program provides both structure and freedom in a safe environment.

An Orderly Sequence

IT IS HELPFUL to know that child development follows a definite sequence. Every area of development takes place step by step. This is true for the development of muscles, language, socialization, intelligence and personality. There are important accomplishments called developmental milestones in every area of development. Consider these examples from motor, language and personality development in turn.

Motor Development refers to the body's ability to move.

Head-to-toe

- A child holds his head without support, sits alone, creeps, crawls, stands on two feet, and walks ... *in that order.* Notice that these accomplishments start at the head and progress, in order, down to the feet. This means it would be foolish to expect a child who cannot yet sit without support to walk, because his body is simply not ready for this yet. Each developmental milestone must be reached in turn.

Large-to-small

- Similarly, a child develops control of large muscles before developing control of small muscles. An infant must practice waving her arms and batting at objects before she will be able to pick them up with her fingers. A preschooler scribbles holding a crayon in the whole palm before being able to hold it between fingers and thumb.

- By remembering the sequence of development, it is possible to observe the child's stage of motor development, know what is possible, and use activities which involve the child's present capabilities. This can provide pleasure and avoid much frustration.

Language Development

- Language development begins long before words are recognized. There are many developmental milestones along the way. A child first coos, then gurgles, makes vowel sounds, consonant sounds, says single words, puts phrases together, forms simple sentences, *in that order.* Each stage needs encouragement and practice. When volunteers can recognize that infants are communicating long before they use words, exciting relationships can result. Pre-verbal infants delight in having the sounds they make repeated back to them. This kind of interaction and practice helps children develop language and enjoy the marvelous reciprocity of human communication.

Children, like adults, understand more words than they use. By age five, most children who have no neurological or hearing impairment have mastered the basics of their native tongue, an amazing accomplishment. Practice with responsive people is important at every stage of language development.

Personality Development

- It is believed that the development of personality and a sense of self also follows a definite sequence. An individual's sense of being a unique, special and capable person does not happen automatically. Human relationships provide powerful feedback at every stage of human development. Erik Erickson defined the sense of trust as the necessary foundation for all healthy personality. Infants need consistent caretaking in order to trust that their basic needs will be met. Otherwise, mistrust can result. Erickson's succeeding stages of personality development involve the individual's inner sense of autonomy, initiative, industry, intimacy vs. contrasting negative developmental possibilities. Erickson defines personality development throughout the life span.

SIMILARLY, JEAN PIAGET defined definite stages of a child's cognitive, or intellectual, development. Arnold Gesell described the whole of child development in detail at every age and stage. These, and other theorists, provide fascinating reading for interested volunteers. It is important to remember that no theory expresses the whole truth, and our knowledge of human development is yet evolving. Reading some of the major theorists can provide enlightenment, and make your work with children more interesting. Ask your supervisor where you may find readings on child development topics which interest you.

Source: Arlene Kiely, Training Consultant, ACCH, Bethesda, MD

Appendix B

Individuality of Temperament

ALTHOUGH DEVELOPMENT FOLLOWS an orderly sequence, individuals vary widely in their temperament or behavioral style. Psychiatrists Stella Chess and Alexander Thomas have defined nine temperamental characteristics which are present at birth. Their work emphasizes the "goodness of fit," or match between parent and child. By recognizing a child's in-born temperament, or preferred behavioral style, parents (and volunteers) are better able to respect individual style and adapt their child-rearing methods accordingly. The nine characteristics Chess and Thomas identified include: Activity Level, Body Rhythms, Threshold of Responsiveness, Intensity, Basic Mood, Adaptability, Approach-Withdrawal, Persistence, and Distractibility. Dr. William Carey has developed an infant temperament scale, as well as questionnaires for preschool teachers, to help determine a child's individual style of behavior. When we understand and respect individual temperament we can avoid pressuring a child, and enable the child to approach situations in the manner comfortable for them.

You can better understand the categories studied by Chess and Thomas if you use them to reflect upon your own temperament, or preferred style of behavior. The following questions invite your reflection, and also help you think about ways to adapt to children's individuality in health care settings.

This is not a test. There are no right or wrong answers. This is a brief review of individual style, or temperament, in the nine categories identified by Chess and Thomas. It should help you consider how to respect individual temperaments in child health care, by taking a look at your own preferred style of behavior.

1. Activity Level

IF PREFERENCE FOR PHYSICAL ACTIVITY could be rated on a scale of 0 to 150, where would you rank yourself? 0 - 150 or, how physically active are you?

0_____150
low activity   high activity

Do you know individuals you would rank at either extreme, below 10, or over 140? This rating is the individual Activity Level, believed to be an inborn characteristic.

APPLICATION: What kinds of activities would work best for children at either extreme? What conflicts might occur if an adult's personal activity level is opposite the child's? How can we recognize and plan ahead for varying needs for physical activity? What problems might thereby be prevented?

2. Body Rhythms

BODY RHYTHMS CAN BE RATED from regular to irregular. Some infants settle quickly after birth into a feeding and sleeping routine. Toilet training is easier when body functions are predictable. At the other extreme, some infants never settle into a predictable pattern, however consistent a parent's attempts at a regular schedule may be. Doubtless you know adults in both extremes, and in the middle. Some people awaken at the same time without an alarm clock. Others never settle into a regular schedule.

APPLICATIONS: Routines in health care settings are more successful with some individuals. For example since not all children will be able to sleep during quiet periods, quiet alternative activities may need to be provided. The routine of the health care setting may be quite different from the schedule at home or the child's internal schedule. Illness and treatments may further alter the child's 'normal' body rhythms.

3. Threshold of Responsiveness

HOW MUCH STIMULATION is needed before you respond? For example, could you sleep through a tornado, or does every sound awaken you? Obviously, sound represents only one kind of stimulus. However, the amount of stimulus needed to cross an individual's threshold can be very low or high. This sensitivity seems to be in-born.

A child, or adult, with a very low stimulus threshold can become easily irritated and tired from too much stimulation. In contrast, an individual with a high stimulus threshold seems to tolerate a great deal more stimulation, and may have difficulty understanding the needs of low-threshold people (or, be unbothered by irritable people!)

APPLICATION: If you know that your own tolerance for stimulation is low, be careful that you do not conclude that more active people are "hyperactive." Also avoid busy, noisy, active group situations, and seek quieter volunteer support. Children can be negatively labeled when these individual differences are unrecognized. When children are sick, it is particularly important to guard against overstimulation and the fatigue and irritability which can result. Rest is needed for healing. Illness may well lower the threshold of responsiveness. The activities in health care settings too frequently violate the needs for quiet, protection from too many people and too many interruptions.

What steps can be taken in this setting to protect children who have low tolerance (or low thresholds) for stimulation?

4. Intensity

HOW STRONGLY DO YOU EXPRESS your personal preferences? For example, if you tasted something unpleasant would you be more likely to swallow it quietly, or spit it out? If you are watching disturbing TV news, would you react silently or express your feelings openly and vigorously?

People differ greatly in the intensity of observable reactions to life experiences. High intensity people may seem more dramatic and colorful. Individuals with low intensity reactions also feel, but do not express feelings as emphatically. Sometimes, opposites attract. At other times they clash when either believes that the other should behave differently.

APPLICATION: Do you feel more attracted to children who express reactions intensely or those who do not? Why? Which type is more like you? Give some examples of situations where behavioral expectations conflict with a child's normal style of low or high intensity. Can you list ways society expects different expressions of intensity in boys and girls?

Children who react with high intensity need their feelings to be supported in a calm manner. Remember also that low intensity children may have emotional needs overlooked because they seem quiet.

Intense reactions are to be expected in health care! Expecting a child to "behave," or not to cry in situations of pain or loss can be harmful. Sound pediatric programs support and normalize feelings with reinforcing statements such as "It's OK to cry when you get a shot. Shots hurt!" or, "Of course you feel sad when you think about home. We want you to get well so you can go home," or "This can be really scary. That's why we want to answer your questions about what worries you." Repression of feelings can lead to depression and despair. The child who is able to actively protest is less likely to become withdrawn or depressed. A strange setting can make even a normally expressive person withdrawn, or, conversely, prompt a usually stable individual to explode. Expressions of intensity may be a healthy response to a sense of danger or discomfort.

5. Basic Mood

WOULD YOU DESCRIBE YOURSELF as basically upbeat and optimistic, usually somewhat negative, or somewhere in between? Whatever description seems to fit, remember that friends and associates might say otherwise! People who are habitually pessimistic and glum are frequently caricatured. A perpetually optimistic person may sometimes seem out of touch with reality, though they will usually be far more popular. It helps to recognize that having a basic mood style is normal. We can learn to accept ourselves and others as we are. Of course, don't assume that every expression of concern or joy reveals a person's basic temperament.

APPLICATION: Real situations can make a basically negative person happy and a basically upbeat person glum. This is especially true in health care settings, which are sources of crisis and stress, far different from normal life. We seldom know what the child or parent is like at home. Volunteers seldom see a child or parent in the context of the whole day's experience, so you must be careful not to judge when you "arrive in the middle of the movie." On the other hand, we should not expect to be able to change any individual's overall basic, inborn characteristic mood. When

Orientation and Training Resources

we know individuals usual patterns, it is easier to accept what is normal for them, as well as note unusual reactions.

6. Adaptability

HOW EASY IS IT FOR YOU to change plans at the last minute? Would you consider yourself very flexible or someone who does not like surprises? (Of course it depends on the circumstances.) However, some individuals can adapt to unplanned change with far less stress than others. They go through life with more ease and are generally a lot easier to get along with. Others need to make careful plans and are most comfortable when plans are followed.

APPLICATION: Compliant children are frequently considered "good" children, because they cause little trouble. They may in fact be genuinely adaptable and "easy to raise." Parents and teachers can be easily tempted to take credit for such children. (On the other hand excessive compliance may sometimes be a result of fear or repression.)

In health care settings, a predictable routine and honest advance explanations about what to expect are critical for all children, even the highly adaptable ones. "Pretty soon it will be clean-up time" is far more helpful and courteous than "Put away the paints now."

According to Chess and Thomas, special clusters of inborn characteristics make some children easier to raise, more adaptable, and other children less easy to raise and less adaptable. While it is unwise to label children, it may be helpful to recognize some of the possible clusters of temperamental characteristics.

The "Easy" Child

The classic "easy to raise" child is one who combines the wonderful qualities of high adaptability, low intensity of reaction, high threshold of responsiveness (or tolerance of stimulation), basic cheerful mood, and moderate to low activity level.

APPLICATION: Childrearing and teaching of such children is usually smooth and pleasant. No wonder parents and teachers are tempted to take credit for the behavior of such children! Such children are easy to get along with, and are generally well-liked by peers and adults alike.

The "Difficult" Child

Consider, however, how different it would be to work with or parent a child who inherited opposite characteristics: very low threshold or tolerance for stimulation, high negative intensity of response, very poor adaptability to any kind of change, basic negative mood and high activity level. There are, indeed, some children who have a more difficult time from birth. If the caretaking adults also share the same combination of difficult characteristics, much conflict can result. However, an adult with similar temperament may be able to provide a more sympathetic environment if they understand from personal experience the things which stress this temperament and how to offer protection. It is very easy for adults to feel frustration and failure when best efforts don't seem to work with this kind of child. Infants who don't like to be held, have difficulty establishing a regular sleep or feeding schedule, react with high negative intensity may induce feelings of failure in parents, staff and volunteers alike.

Children with such temperament may be further stressed because they feel unable to "settle down." They may feel a sense of shame or isolation when their reactions seem to cause negative responses from adults and peers.

APPLICATION: "Difficult" children require a great deal of ingenuity and patience from adults. Most people naturally prefer the satisfaction of working with "easy" children. In health care settings, the difficult child may be the one most in need of support, extra reassurance, advance preparation, reduction of stimuli, predictable routines, and calm acceptance. Staff may also need to take turns with them!

It is not only acceptable, but important to acknowledge that not all children are likeable, that some are especially appealing and popular, and that different adults have different preferences. What must be avoided is showing open favoritism, making some children feel special and others left out. Labeling children as "difficult" or "easy" can also serve as a self-fulfilling prophecy. Behaviors which seem "difficult" to some adults may not be "difficult" for others at all.

It is most unfortunate when adults compete to work with "favorite" children, or feel that they are the only person who understands a particular child. Keeping in touch with feelings, discussing them with appropriate staff, and planning to meet the needs of all children without showing favoritism is essential. Children, likewise respond differently to adults. Assignments can frequently be made based on previous successful interactions. Flexible volunteers who are willing to take on difficult assignments are an asset to any program.

7. Approach/Withdrawal — Preferences

THIS CHARACTERISTIC STUDIED by Chess and Thomas includes a subcategory of normal behavior identified as "Slow to Warm Up." Consider your own preferred style. Do you plunge enthusiastically into new situations? Do you prefer to hold back and proceed with caution before entering into a new experience?

APPLICATION: Children, too, have a natural preferred style which should be respected. It serves no purpose to assume that friendly children are more socially mature and shy children somehow deficient. The "slow to warm up" child is the one who takes time to become fully integrated into a group, but does eventually do so. Adults frequently take credit for such success, not realizing that this is a life-long pattern which is normal for that individual. This temperamental pattern differs from that of individuals whose life-long style is to remain withdrawn even after long experience in a group.

Two other characteristics of individual temperament may seem mutually exclusive, but are not. They are:

8. & 9. Persistence and Distractibility

HOW WOULD YOU RATE your persistence, or ability to stick with a task from start to finish? Is persistence natural, or does it require effort? Do you prefer to complete one task before beginning another, or are you energized by variety?

Can you be easily distracted from a task? How bothersome are distractions? Do they get you permanently off the track? Not affect you at all? Affect your concentration only briefly? It is possible to be distractible, yet still be persistent in completing a task.

APPLICATION: Children with high persistence and low distractibility can focus on either work or play in all kinds of surroundings. Children with low persistence and high distractibility have more trouble focusing on either play or learning, regardless of their talents or intelligence. They do better when distractions are minimized. In general, a child's attention span increases with age. Some individuals, however, have life-long problems with both persistence and distractibility. Parents and teachers alike have frustrations nurturing accomplishments of such children. These individuals may feel frustrated and develop low self-esteem, despite often considerable abilities.

In health care settings, it should be recognized that a child's stress and hidden fears may interfere with the normal ability to persist or concentrate, even in play. Trained staff are alert to fears and misconceptions which may be revealed through play. Freedom of choice in play helps reduce stress.

Distractible children may flit from activity to activity. As long as this does not disturb others, it may sometimes be acceptable, even helpful to the child. However, protecting such children from the interruptions of sights and sounds helps them focus on an activity and experience the pleasure of completing a game or craft. Even very persistent children can be highly frustrated when there is insufficient time allowed to complete an activity.

Conclusion

INDIVIDUALS INTERESTED in further readings on temperament should consult the numerous works of Stella Chess, M.D., and Alexander Thomas, M.D., and those of William Carey, M.D. In addition, Isabell Myers Briggs has developed a Personality Type Inventory. The Myers-Briggs inventories are designed for adults, but applications have been made to childhood characteristics. Understanding and respecting individuality is the key to application of all personality and temperament categorizations.

Source: Arlene Kiely, Training Consultant, ACCH, Bethesda, MD

Appendix B

Understanding Personal Preferences

IT IS IMPORTANT FOR VOLUNTEERS to be aware of their own reactions and how these can influence judgment and performance. It is perfectly natural that volunteers, staff, and parents will find some children or situations more appealing than others. Perhaps a first rule of remaining open is: know thyself!

The following exercise gives you an opportunity to be aware of your own preferences.

INSTRUCTIONS: Read through all of the following descriptions of children. Imagine you are invited to choose those children you would most prefer to work with. Then, rank your first through last choice of assignment by placing a number, 1-6, opposite each description below. THERE ARE NO RIGHT OR WRONG ANSWERS.

_____Bobby is a 4-month-old infant hospitalized with acute diarrhea. He is alert, friendly, and sociable.

_____Jackie is an 8-month-old girl who does not like to be held. When taken to the playroom she seems tense, and turns away when toddlers approach her. Feeding is difficult.

_____Tommy is a very active 2-year-old who likes to run up and down the hall. He has a short attention span. He says a few words, often likes to hit and say "no."

_____Sally is a 4-year-old with mental retardation. She likes to rock and hum to herself. She turns book pages without looking at the pictures. She has no visitors.

_____Ted is a bright second grader who collects baseball cards and small cars. He likes Batman and Superman and drawing pictures. He has leukemia.

_____Maureen is a 13-year-old girl who broke her leg in a bike accident. She seems bossy to other children. She is very critical of hospital routines and frequently expresses intense dislike for certain staff.

Orientation and Training Resources

- Briefly list the reasons for your preference ranking. Which child would you most prefer to work with? Why? List at least three reasons.
- Which child was least appealing? Why? Give at least three reasons.
- Why might someone else's first choice be the child you least preferred? Why might someone else least prefer your first choice?

Commentary

Obviously, there are no right or wrong choices. It is important to be aware, however, of the factors which often determine your personal preferences for certain children.

Preferences might be based on: personal appeal, comfort with a certain age level, knowledge of activities which have a chance of success, a sense of challenge in relating to a difficult child or situation, a sense of obligation, pity, or fear of failure.

- What factors influenced your choices?
- Which are assets?
- What might help you overcome those things which make you less comfortable working with certain kinds of children and situations?
- What questions do you need to ask your supervisor for guidance?

You will not always be able to volunteer with the children whose behaviors, age levels, or situations are most appealing. Being able to work where needed, to adapt to the changing needs of the program is one of the most valuable and appreciated contributions a volunteer can make. By remaining open to new challenges, many volunteers have discovered hidden strengths and developed new skills in situations where they felt initially uncomfortable. It is important to seek guidance in situations where you feel less than comfortable. This will improve your knowledge, your skill, your sense of satisfaction, and your contributions to children, parents and staff alike.

Source: Arlene Kiely, Training Consultant, ACCH, Bethesda, MD
Adapted from: Roxane Kaufmann, Georgetown Child Development Center, Washington, DC

Appendix B

Observing and Playing with Children

As you spend time with children you will have many opportunities to see how they play and act, both alone and with others. The following information is given to help you report your observations to staff. The more accurate the information you give us about the children, the better able we are to understand and help them.

We are interested in the child's motor, cognitive, language and affective development. We are interested in how the child relates to others and what his play is like. We are interested in how he copes with potentially stressful situations.

Motor Development

MOTOR DEVELOPMENT INCLUDES gross and fine motor skills. Gross motor skills are the child's abilities in using large muscles for crawling, climbing, walking, running, bike pedaling, ball throwing and kicking, etc.

Fine motor skills involve the child's small muscle abilities, using fingers to pick up small objects, string beads, do needlework, build towers, make constructions or place puzzle pieces correctly. How does the child use his body and hands? Is she graceful or awkward? Can he generally do what he attempts?

Cognitive Development

COGNITIVE DEVELOPMENT refers to the child's intellectual abilities. Intellectual abilities include problem solving, creativity, retaining and retrieving of information.

Problem solving and creativity both involve looking at a situation in a new way. Does the child experiment with situations until he comes up with a solution? Retaining and retrieving information are important aspects to learning. How much does the child seem to know, understand and remember? Is the child curious, interested in exploring his surroundings? Does the child use fantasy and imagination in his play?

Language Development

LANGUAGE DEVELOPMENT is composed of both receptive and expressive language skills. Receptive language is what the child understands. Can he do what you request of him? Does she respond to what you say? Expressive language is what the child can communicate. How extensive is his vocabulary? Does he speak easily or haltingly? Can her speech be understood? What about his non-verbal communication? What does she convey by gesture, posture, expression or other body language?

Affective Development

AFFECTIVE DEVELOPMENT involves the child's feelings and emotions. How the child behaves can help us to understand how the child may be feeling. Each child's temperament is different and each child will react in his own way to differing situations. It is important not to label children but instead to observe their individual behaviors in each situation. For example, a child is not "spoiled, loving, or violent," but instead may sometimes demonstrate behaviors like whining, giving affection or showing anger. Observe what the child does when he seems angry, uncertain or overwhelmed. How does the child indicate pleasure or fear? Does the child seem spontaneous, inhibited, impulsive? What kind of inner- or self-control does the child demonstrate?

The Child's Relationships

HOW DOES THE CHILD RELATE TO OTHERS? Does he socialize easily, hang back from the group or seem to prefer to be alone? What are his relationships with his parents like? Does he include them in his play, ignore them, cling to them or seem to be angry with them? How does the child relate to you, to other staff? Does he seek affection, test limits, ask for help? How does he relate to the other children? Does he play side by side or engage in cooperative group play? Is she a leader or a follower? How does he feel about winning and losing? Is he competitive?

The Child's Play

WHAT IS THE CHILD'S PLAY LIKE? How long is his attention span? Does he stay absorbed in his play or move quickly from one activity to the next? Do some activities hold his attention longer than others? Which? Is he interested in trying new experiences? How complicated and elaborate is his play? Does he approach projects creatively or in a constrained manner? Do certain themes and ideas recur in play, in art, or in conversation?

The Child's Coping Skills

HOW DOES THE CHILD HANDLE TRANSITIONS? How does he act when moving from one activity to another? Does he quickly decide what he wants to do? Does he seem at loose ends? Does he need time and/or help to become reinvolved?

How does the child deal with separations? How does he act when his parents leave? How does the child separate from you? Does he cry, act offhand, get angry, or ignore his parents or you? Does he try various methods to get the adult to stay? What are they? How does he respond to his doctors and nurses? Does he act afraid or seem relaxed with them? Does he behave differently with them at different times? When and how? How does the child react to medical procedures? Does the child seem to have strategies that help him to cope with stressful situations? For example, does he use humor, find comfort in a security blanket, ask lots of questions or imagine himself in a more pleasant setting?

Developing Relationships
Approaching Children and Families

WHEN THE PLAY SESSION BEGINS you may be assigned to a child whom you will invite to come to the playroom. Your supervisor may ask you to check with the child's nurse first to be sure that the child is able to come to the playroom. You may be assigned to play with a child who must stay in his room because he requires isolation or bedrest. The nurse and your supervisor will tell you what you are expected to do to get ready to play with the child. Toys and materials for the child in isolation may need to be handled in a special way to prevent the spreading of germs.

When you first approach the child tell him your name and that you are from the playroom. Children need to know who you are and why you are coming to see them. If you are inviting the child to the playroom let the child choose if he wants to come or not. If you have been assigned to a child who must remain in his room let him choose if he wants you to stay and play. If the child doesn't want to play he is not rejecting you. He may not feel well. He may just like the chance to say no. You may offer to bring a toy or activity to the child and to check back with him later.

If parents are present include them in your conversation when you introduce yourself to the child. Sometimes the parent and child want to play together and only want you to bring them something to do. Sometimes parents want you to play with their child while they go eat or rest. If your supervisor has said you are not needed in the playroom you can stay and play in the child's room. If you are inviting the child to come to the playroom let his parents know they are welcome there too.

Talking with Children and Families

IN YOUR CONVERSATIONS with a child let him take the lead. Allow the child to choose how much he wants to talk and what he wants to talk about. Be an attentive listener. Whenever possible, postpone adult conversations until your involvement with the child is over. Try to avoid asking the child questions about himself or telling him information about yourself. Keep your responses focused on the child's interests in such a way that allows for further discussion if the child wants. For example, a child may tell you that she had surgery last week. Rather than saying that you also had surgery once or asking what the surgery was for, you can respond by saying, "Last week?" or "Really?" responses which indicate that you are interested but do not require the child to either focus on your experience or reveal more of hers than she may feel comfortable to do.

Often children want to take their time before confiding information about their situation. Some may feel unable to talk about it at all.

It is important that you be honest and reliable in what you say to the children, Only tell children you will return to see them or that something won't hurt if you know that is true. Even if information is difficult to give and receive, honest statements build the child's trust in you. It is not your role to give the child information about his medical condition. If the child asks you questions that you cannot or should not answer, tell him that you will try to find someone to talk with him and then refer the questions to your supervisor.

You can help children and their families preserve their privacy. Information about patients should be discussed by you only in private with child development staff or in "rounds." If an adult asks you what is wrong with a child you can reply that you are unable to say or that you do not know. Other potentially intrusive questions to be aware of include asking what the child is doing, making or thinking. Even, "What grade are you in in school?" can be an uncomfortable question for a child whose illness has prevented his keeping up with his class. Sometimes one child will ask why another child is in the hospital. Often this question is asked about a child with visible problems and reflects the questioner's anxiety about the same things happening to him. If the child being asked about heard the questions, you can ask him if he would like to answer. If he chooses not to, you can tell the questioner that each child is here so his doctors can help him and that children are in the hospital for many different reasons. This response should provide some reassurance for the questioner without excluding or intruding any more on the child being asked about.

It is important to be very cautious about using humor with children. Children can easily misunderstand adult humor. For example, one child was kidded by his doctor who said that he saw dinosaurs inside the child's ears during an examination. Later the child expressed a great deal of concern about getting the dinosaurs removed.

When you are playing with children you will sometimes have to help them to limit certain behaviors. You do not want to let children do anything to hurt themselves or others. You may need to help them to control very noisy or active play. Sometimes volunteers and students are reluctant to intervene because they think the children won't like them if their behaviors are limited. Sometimes volunteers and students are unsure if certain behaviors are an acceptable expression of the child's feelings or not. Your supervisor can help you to learn more about limit setting. Children usually respond positively when their behaviors need to be limited. It is reassuring to children to know that the adults will not let them get out of control.

When setting limits it is important that you avoid moralistic and judgmental statements to children. Statements like, "That's not nice," may be aimed at changing a child's behavior but can also damage his self-esteem. If the child's behavior is unacceptable it is preferable to say simply, "I don't want you to do that," and tell him why. This approach lets the child know what kind of behavior you expect from him without making him feel bad.

You can help patients and families also by not sharing your own medical experiences and advice with them. They need to focus on their own situation and rely on the expertise of the medical staff. Instead, talk with your supervisor about any observations or concerns you may have.

Conversations can be centered around the child's activity or happenings in the room. Often there will be times when you need not say anything. Your presence, a smile, a look of interest will be just what the child needs.

Playing with Children

WHEREVER YOU ARE PLAYING with children in the hospital there are some concepts to be aware of that can help you to provide the kind of relationship that pediatric patients can benefit from.

Within the limits of safety and concern for others, children should be allowed to choose and direct their play. In many aspects of their hospitalization children cannot have choices about what is happening to them. Choice in play allows them control over what they are doing and lets them select the activities that can best meet their needs at the time. The child may want you to participate in his play. He may become involved by himself and just want your company. If he does want you to participate let him be the one in charge. You may suggest certain activities if he is not sure what he wants to do but let him make the choice and be the leader in the play. If a child asks you for help try to suggest ways he can help himself. For example, a child may ask you to draw a picture of a dog. You can ask if he would draw the head first or what the ears would look like. Often questions like these are enough to help the child to begin his own drawing. You might find a picture of a dog in a book or magazine to help the child to get started.

Sometimes it is appropriate to do something for a child but try to help him to help himself first. Perhaps your repositioning one puzzle piece can help a child to continue to work successfully on completing a puzzle. This kind of approach helps to build the child's confidence and self-esteem. In dramatic play also let the child determine the content of the play. If a child invites you to the medical play table, let him direct the play, deciding what your illness is, what treatment is necessary and how to carry it out. In this way you can learn about the child's ideas and he can play out his conceptualization of the medical procedures he is reenacting. As a play patient you can enter the play putting yourself in the child's place or role modeling for the child. "I don't like shots. I like to know what's happening." These kinds of responses can validate the child's feelings and help him learn to ask questions about what is happening to him.

Orientation and Training Resources

In the Playroom Setting

THE PLAYROOM PROVIDES children an environment in which they can pursue familiar, pleasurable activities. You can help in several ways to keep the experience as meaningful as possible.

We ask that no procedures or examinations that are upsetting to the child be done in the playroom. We ask the hospital staff to take the child out of the playroom when these events must occur. This rule preserves the relaxed atmosphere of the playroom setting. Sometimes doctors will come in to listen to a child's chest with a stethoscope or briefly examine a bandage. Sometimes a nurse will enter to give a child a pill. If it is not upsetting to the child they are welcome to do so since then the child does not have to stop his play to leave the room. We encourage adults in the playroom to sit down and play with or watch the child at play. We encourage conversation involving the child, preferring that adult conversations be postponed or engaged in outside of the playroom.

Parents are welcome to leave their child in the playroom as long as there is enough help to adequately supervise the child. If not the parents will either need to stay or to return the child to his room until someone is free to play with him.

Often children will come to the playroom with I.V.s or other medical apparatus. It is the nurses responsibility to check patients' medical equipment but you can help the child if you learn when the nurse's assistance is needed. Your supervisor can give you this information.

The playroom setting will be appealing to children if materials are presented in an attractive way. You can help to maintain an appealing environment by cleaning up and resetting work areas after a child is finished there. For example, when a child has finished an art project, you can move the completed work to the counter and straighten up the table, replenishing materials if necessary.

It is important to be aware of what is happening in all areas of the playroom. If you are involved with a patient and are unable to give help that is needed elsewhere in the playroom you can ask another student or volunteer to help out instead.

Giving a "Five minutes until closing" announcement helps to prepare children for the playroom's closing. Often taking a toy or activity back to his room can help the child to leave the playroom more easily.

Source: Pediatric Volunteers' and Students', Child Development Handbook, Susan V. Clark, M.A., Child Development Specialist, Department of Child Development Services, UCLA Medical Center, Los Angeles, CA

Functions of Play in Health Care Settings

- Allows a child freedom of choice. This is especially needed when so much health care treatment is not freely chosen. When a child rejects an activity, he has been allowed to experience some control.

- Encourages engagement in activities which are personally satisfying.

- Permits control of and manipulation of materials (this can be especially satisfying in settings where so much seems to be done to children.)

- Allows a safe acting out of aggressive and hostile feelings. Feelings are facts. Safe expression in play helps release tension and can also reveal a child's misconceptions about treatment and care. Professional staff can intervene appropriately.

- Imaginative play allows imitation, critique, commentary, and trying out of adult roles. It can also reveal a child's frequently accurate and humorous perspective on adult behaviors.

- Provides opportunities for socialization.

- Can be a pleasant diversion from worry and stress.

- Mastering a game, skill, or art project can provide a sense of accomplishment.

- Arts and crafts made for self, family, or friends enable pride in creativity.

- Observing, exploring, and manipulating materials is the beginning of scientific inquiry.

Source: Arlene Kiely, Training Consultant, ACCH, Bethesda, MD

Self-Orientation: Play in This Setting

Instructions: You can help orient yourself to this setting by learning the answers to each of the following questions:

- What is the schedule for play and recreational activities?

- How do I choose children to work with?

- When might I work with groups, individuals, or with children who are in protective isolation?

- What play equipment is available here?

- If there are indoor and outdoor play areas, what do I need to know about each, in finding answers to the following questions? Where is it kept? What are storage rules?

- What are the guidelines for setting up the play area?

Appendix B

- What are guidelines for clean-up and closing the play area?

- How do volunteers obtain play materials?

- What are the safety requirements?

- How are toys cleaned?

- What restrictions apply, as in taking play materials into places where children may be in protective isolation?

- What kind of materials can volunteers bring in? Are there any precautions?

- What else do I need to ask the supervisor about play?

Source: Arlene Kiely, Training Consultant, ACCH, Bethesda, MD

Exercise: What is Play?

Instructions: Take an inventory of play by completing the following. Enjoy!

1. List ten activities you enjoy in your leisure time:

2. "Play is ..." (complete with as many words as possible)

3. What does play or recreation do for you personally?

4. List five activities other people enjoy which have no appeal for you:

5. Based on the above, what criteria must play satisfy for you?

6. What other functions might play serve for other types of people?

Appendix B

7. Compare different individuals' preferences for:
   — solo activities vs. group activities
   — non-competitive vs. competitive activities
   — structured vs. non-structured
   — physical vs. non-physical
   — active vs. passive
   — activities which involve special skill or talent
   — activities which involve special equipment
   — sports
   — music
   — arts
   — crafts

8. What, if any, are the universal characteristics of play? (Two which have been identified are freedom of choice and pleasure.)

9. What are some additional functions of play in health care settings?

As you volunteer and facilitate the play of children, be mindful not only of the individuality of choice, but the need of each individual to move at their own pace. Children frequently are satisfied to watch the play of others. Observation can be a form of engagement.

If a child seems hesitant, it may be helpful to say to a child, "Maybe you'd just like to watch for a while." Or, "You can watch and then decide what you'd like to do when you're ready."

If a child seems especially interested in an activity, invite participation. Some children feel a need for invitation and permission to participate in play in a place that is unfamiliar.

Source: Arlene Kiely, Training Consultant, ACCH, Bethesda, MD

Orientation and Training Resources

List of Suggested Play Materials

According to Age and Developmental Stages

The First Year

Here, in what Piaget calls the sensorimotor phase of human development, the infant progresses from instinctual reflexes (e.g., closing the hand around an object placed in it) to coordinated controlled muscle movements. Through exploration of his environment, he proceeds to "practice play," delighted repetition of an action which he himself has caused. So he needs:

Things to Look at:...
- Crib mobiles and bright dangling objects
- Wood or plastic-framed steel mirror
- Cloth or heavy cardboard picture books

Things to Touch, Grasp, Shake, Manipulate...
- Rattles (4 months +)
- Small soft animals or dolls (4 months +)
- Soft rubber squeeze toys (1 year)
- Ball — woolly or foam with contoured shape (4 months +)
- Plastic disks on chain, plastic spoons (4 months +)
- Smooth clothespin
- Household sponge
- Floating bath toys (6 months +)
- Plastic beads and blocks
- Nesting and stacking color toys (9 months +)

Things to Listen to...
- Ticking clock
- Music box or musical mobile
- Wind chimes

Things to Taste and Chew...
- Rubber or plastic teething rings (5 months)

Appendix B

Twelve to Twenty-four Months

A creeping, crawling, staggering, walking, climbing period in the course of which, to use Erik Erikson's terms, the child either develops basic trust and confidence or, if discouraged from active inquiry, lapses into self-doubt. Now he wants:

Things That Move...

- Pull and push toys, preferably those that clatter or jangle
- Large, foot-propelled riding toys — tractor, locomotive, horse, etc.
- Small rocking chair

Things to Build with and Manipulate...

- Small blocks
- Nesting blocks
- Drop-the-block-through-the-hole-type toys
- Pounding bench — hammer and pegs
- Mud and sand equipment — pail, shovel, spoons, scoops, molds
- Bean bag

Things to Love...

- Soft dolls and stuffed animals

Two to Three Years

The child adds to earlier interests a passion for "symbolic play" just-pretending, which helps him assimilate new knowledge, as practice play helped him assimilate new physical skills.

Things for Make-believe...

- Dolls, doll accessories — blankets, bed, carriage, tea set, telephone
- Housekeeping materials — toy broom, dusters, pots and pans, little table and chairs, iron
- Wheeled vehicles — fire engine, cars, trucks — large and small
- Dress-up clothes

Things to Make the Fingers Work...

- Large beads to string (2½ years +)
- Books and toys that involve buttoning, lacing, fitting interlocking parts (3 years +)
- Good sturdy blocks (2 years +)
- Blunt scissors and construction paper (3 years +)
- Dress-me dolls and zippers, buckles, snaps, etc.
- Small rubber balls

- Blackboard and chalk
- Crayons, fingerpaints, clay
- Bubbles

Thinking Things

- Wooden puzzles with big pieces (2½ years +)
- Lift-out puzzles with easily-identifiable objects that can be removed, played with, and refitted
- Lotto cards for simple matching (3 years)
- Plastic or metal letters and numbers; magnetized ones are nice to use on the refrigerator door (2½ years +)

Three to Four Years

Three is a plateau of relative calm, cheerfulness, cooperation, and sociability. The three-year-old has discovered that patience sometimes works better than furious attack; he knows the power of language. Now he will work, seriously and carefully, at any skill promising a surer control of his world. He wants materials he can use in his own way (sand, clay, blocks, wood) and also those he can use in distinctively adult ways. Carrying over many of the toddler toys, he also enjoys:

- Felt pens
- Poster paints, fingerpaints, easel
- Color and shape and design materials (bits of interestingly-shaped plastic or felt that adhere to a larger picture surface)
- Block printing and equipment
- Solid child-size hammer, large nails, soft wood
- Wagon, wheelbarrow, tricycle
- Simple music makers — drum, tambourine, castanets, triangle, rhythm sticks, maracas
- Phonograph and records
- Materials for playing house, store, train

Four to Five Years

Four is off-balance again, struggling to be "it." Four is tempestuous and extreme (Gessell's label is "out of bounds") battering at whatever opposes his will. His imagination and energy reach new heights. He needs play materials that take up this energy and direct it constructively.

- Workbench with saw, vise, screwdriver, wrench — used under supervision
- Fit-together construction toys — Tinkertoy, Bristle blocks, etc.
- Miniature people, animals, vehicles for block play
- Dress-ups for particular occupations — nurse, policeman, astronaut, fireman, carpenter

- Board games — simple, Snakes and Ladders, Candyland, etc.
- Puzzles, picture lotto
- Cooking equipment
- Kite
- Wheels, all kinds: trucks, bulldozers, tractors, trains
- Flashlight

Five to Six Years

The kindergartener is a responsible citizen. He handles tools, problems, his own emotions with new assurance; he makes plans. For him, the best play involves other children and a clear relationship with the real world. New strong interests are:

- Science materials—magnet, magnifying glass, flashlight, stethoscope, clocks and cars with see-through mechanism
- Cameras, simple instamatic
- Modeling materials that dry or bake to a permanent finish
- Dolls with convincing accessories
- Doll houses with furniture, people
- Miniature forts, filling stations, farms
- Crafts involving small-muscle coordination — loop looms, spool knitting, simple sewing, stringing beads
- Jigsaw puzzle
- Skipping rope, roller skates, ice skates

Six to Seven Years

Six is active and social, eager for those skills which confer status in a group. "Toys" become less important than the paraphernalia of sport and games.

- Skipping rope
- Two-wheel bicycle
- Baseball equipment
- Fishing tackle
- Jacks, marbles, tops
- Board games, dominos
- Doctor and nurse accessories
- Trains with tracks, switches, signals
- Paperdolls
- Puppets and puppet theater
- Marionettes
- Pedometer, stilts
- Croquet set

- Gyroscope
- Field glasses
- Craft materials, moderately advanced - Formafilm
- Simple erector sets

Seven to Eight Years

Seven-year-olds like systems and rules, admire physical prowess. They engage in elaborate imaginative play, more sustained than earlier "let's pretend" and welcome realistic equipment suitable for astronauts or queens. A few intense interests often now replace the earlier range of activities.

- Costumes and accessories of all sorts
- Board games depending on skill as well as luck — checkers, Monopoly
- Card games
- Puzzles and skill-teasers, yo-yo
- Simple magic tricks
- Walkie-talkie
- Collector's equipment — coin folders, butterfly net, stamp books
- Model airplanes

Eight to Twelve Years

This is an age of passionate interest in "how things work" and "how to make things." It's the time, as Ruth Hartley says, for "tabletop physics and kitchen chemistry." Play materials now should call forth energy, inventiveness, independence and orderly, systematic activity.

- Craft materials, fairly advanced — weaving, embroidery, metalcraft, woodcarving
- More difficult board games — Othello, chess
- Magic stunts and tricks
- Compass
- Materials for electromagnetic experiments
- Plywood, coping saw, plane
- Plastic and paper sculpture materials
- Telescope, microscope
- Sport supplies — tennis, ping-pong, badminton
- Model car kits
- Electronic and computer games

Thirteen + Years

Adolescents undergo dramatic physical and mental change in a short period of time. At no other time in life are feelings about the self (self-esteem) so closely tied to feelings about the body (body image). One of the most obvious social changes is the initiation of serious interest in and interactions with young people of the opposite sex. The most important mental change is the growth in capacity for abstract thinking. At the same time comes the realization that choices need to be made towards education, career and long-lasting friendships.

- Arts and crafts
- Games — board games, packs of cards, ping-pong, pool electronic and computer games
- Movies — VCR
- Music — tape recorder and cassettes
- Puzzles — advanced

Source: Manual for Child Life Volunteers, Schneider Children's Hospital, Long Island Jewish Medical Center, New Hyde Park, NY

Orientation and Training Resources

Exercise: Play Activities Review

List several good activities for individual play with:

— an infant

— a toddler

— a pre-schooler

— a school-age child

— an adolescent

— a child confined to a wheelchair

— a child confined to bed

— a child receiving IV

What are good group activities for children at different stages of development?

— for pre-schoolers

— for school-aged children

— for adolescents

Source: Arlene Kiely, Training Consultant, ACCH, Bethesda, MD

Appendix B

Planning Age-Appropriate Play:
Volunteer Exercise

How much do you already know about child development and the kinds of play which are appropriate at different ages? How attentive and adaptable can you be to special circumstances in health care? The following exercise will help you to review child development and age-appropriate play, as well as to plan some creative adapting to special circumstances.

Individual Instructions: Imagine yourself volunteering with each of the children described below. Answer as best you can. Then, use the discussion guide on the following page for review with your supervisor or group.

Group Instructions: Give each individual or small group one situation to discuss and share, in turn, with the larger group. See discussion leader's guide, page B64.

1) A four-month-old infant hospitalized for severe diarrhea. Her right arm is restrained because of an IV.

   a. development expected at this age:

   b. appropriate play activities:

   c. any special considerations:

2) An eleven-month-old boy hospitalized with failure to thrive.

   a. development expected at this age:

   b. appropriate play activities:

   c. any special considerations:

3) An eighteen-month-old girl being treated for swallowing a household product.

   a. development expected at this age:

   b. appropriate play activities:

   c. any special considerations:

4) A four-year-old boy who has had an emergency appendectomy.

   a. development expected at this age:

   b. appropriate play activities:

   c. any special considerations:

5) A six-year-old in his fifth week of intravenous treatment for a bone infection.

   a. development expected at this age:

   b. appropriate play activities:

   c. any special considerations:

6) An eleven-year-old girl who has lost her hair as a result of treatment for leukemia.

   a. development expected at this age:

   b. appropriate play activities:

   c. any special considerations:

7) A sixteen-year-old deaf boy hospitalized with newly-diagnosed diabetes.

   a. development expected at this age:

   b. appropriate play activities:

   c. any special considerations:

Source: Arlene Kiely, Training Consultant, ACCH, Bethesda, MD

Appendix B

Planning Age-Appropriate Play:
Instructor's Guide

These situations are intended to highlight the importance of keeping an open mind, being willing to be flexible, and above all, the importance of sharing questions and concerns with the appropriate staff supervisor. Ask each group to report in turn on the situations (pages B62-63). Additional questions may include:

Situation 1:

A four-month-old infant hospitalized for severe diarrhea. Her right arm is restrained because of an IV.

 a. When, why, and how are restraints used?
 b. How can the child's frustration be minimized?
 c. Can a volunteer hold an infant who is receiving an IV? If so, demonstrate how this may be done safely.
 d. What do volunteers need to know about IV administration?
 e. Is it safe to hold a child who has diarrhea? How can this be done? What other precautions need to be observed?
 f. What kinds of visual, auditory, and tactile stimuli/activities might work with this infant?

Situation 2:

An eleven-month-old boy hospitalized with failure to thrive.

 a. What is failure to thrive? What is the difference between a biological (organic) failure and a psychological (psychogenic) cause?
 b. How can volunteers avoid being judgmental of parental relationships? How can they be supportive?
 c. How do adults learn to read infants' cues and respond? What infant behaviors signal stress and overstimulation, a need to withdraw? What behaviors signal readiness for stimulation and interaction?
 d. How are feeding protocols established?
 e. Why are consistent relationships important in early infancy? How does trust develop? How does an institution attend to the need for consistency in caretaking?

Situation 3:

An eighteen-month-old girl being treated for swallowing a household product.

a. Why is safety a primary concern in working with toddlers? What kinds of precautions are needed?
b. How can volunteers and staff be sensitive to parents' feelings? What feelings are these parents likely to have? What kind of additional support might they need?

Situation 4:

A four-year-old boy who has had an emergency appendectomy.

a. What are the possible psychological complications from emergency surgery? For the child? For the family?
b. What makes a planned admission better?
c. Why is four a particularly vulnerable age for surgery of any kind?
d. What is known about psychosexual development and castration fears?
e. How can a knowledge of common age level fears guide caretaking and support?

Situation 5:

A six-year-old in his fifth week of intravenous treatment for a bone infection.

a. What are the common interests and fears of school-aged children?
b. What might be some concerns of a child who is hospitalized for a long time?
c. What conversational topics might be most appreciated? What activities?
d. What kinds of negative feelings about the experience might be expected? How can these be supported?

Situation 6:

An eleven-year-old girl who has lost her hair as a result of treatment for leukemia.

a. How is body image essential to one's self-esteem?
b. Why is concern over body image particularly strong at this age?
c. What activities would be helpful?
d. What other fears might this child have?
e. What kinds of support are available for concerns about dying?

Situation 7:

A sixteen-year-old deaf boy hospitalized with newly diagnosed diabetes.

a. What are the ways that hearing people communicate with deaf people?
b. How are deaf people usually regarded and treated by the hearing culture?
c. What is the meaning of diabetes to this young man?
d. How will staff promote his autonomy and self-control in management of his eating?
e. What kinds of feelings might be expected?
f. How can a volunteer be most supportive?

Source: Arlene B. Kiely, Training Consultant, ACCH, Bethesda, Md.

Guidelines for Expressive Arts With Children

Choices

- Provide a wide variety of safe materials and activities (art, music, movement, poetry, story-writing, drama).

- Provide a comfortable, clean space. Some, but not all, children need uncluttered work space.

- Offer an abundant supply of materials. When quantities are limited, some children may feel left out, or restricted in their choices.

- Encourage freedom of choice of materials, methods, and activities, as well as opportunities for mixing media and activities.

Timing

- Assure plenty of time for explorations, time for each child to work at own pace.

- Try not to interrupt a child absorbed in the creative process.

- Give plenty of warning when time is running out . . . "Pretty soon it will be time for clean up."

- If there is insufficient time to finish, provide a time to finish later, a place to store materials, or give extra materials to take home.

Presentation

- Encourage the individual creative process, rather than prescribed products or activities. (Example: Blank paper is usually more inviting than a coloring book.)

- Remember that some children will be inhibited by a demonstration, and think "I can't do that."

Encouraging Creativity

- Say "You can think of lots of different ways to do it." . . . "You can do it any way you like." . . . "There is no right or wrong way."

- Invite the child to "Tell me about it" instead of asking "What is that?"

- Comment favorably on the artist's choices. Say "You used some interesting shapes." . . . "I like the way you used the colors." . . . "You played that very softly." . . . "That's a special arm motion."

- Avoid comparing one child's work with another. However, when children make comparisons, say "Isn't it interesting that everyone has their own special way to be an artist (dancer, poet, story-teller, musician)?"

- Help each child decide how, or if, they wish to share, display or save their work.

Source: Arlene B. Kiely, Training Consultant, ACCH, Bethesda, Md

Appendix B

caring for kids

Guidelines for Interacting with Children and Adolescents in Health Care Settings

Remember:

- ☐ **To Be at the Child's Eye Level**
  It is often scary for young children in a strange environment to have people tower over them.

- ☐ **To Introduce Yourself to the Patient and Family**
  To inititally introduce yourself and your role in the hospital.

- ☐ **To Be Honest**
  Hiding the truth from children, even with the best of intentions, results in the child losing trust in hospital personnel.

- ☐ **To Respect Expressions of Emotion**
  Crying and anger are normal. The child will feel and cope better if encouraged to express these emotions.

- ☐ **To Give the Child Real Choices**
  If the child can choose between juice or water to drink with their medication, great! However, the child has no choice about taking his medication, so do not offer one.

- ☐ **To Support the Relationship Between the Child and Family**
  All children, including teens, need family support. Include the family in decisions and problem solving.

- ☐ **To Respect the Child's Right for Privacy**
  Everyone needs their own space, both physically and emotionally. Adolescents, in particular, are sensitive to violations of this basic human right.

- ☐ **All Children Are Not Raised the Same**
  Our children come from many different backgrounds and cultures. Therefore, do not expect everyone to use the same child rearing techniques.

- ☐ **To Administer Painful Procedures in the Treatment Room**
  Playrooms, activity rooms and patient rooms should be "safe" places for children.

- ☐ **A Smile is Contagious**
  Maintain a positive attitude. A friendly approach is always more effective.

Avoid:

- ☐ **Comparing a Child to Others**
  Comparisons such as, "You should be able to do this. Sandy is younger than you and can do it", can destroy a child's self-esteem.

- ☐ **Treating Children As Pets**
  Children will indicate either verbally or physically when they need to receive some physical comfort.

- ☐ **Pitying**
  People need supporting care, not gushy sympathy.

- ☐ **Talking Down to Children**
  Treat children appropriately for their age. Appearance can be deceiving so know the age and developmental abilities of your patient.

- ☐ **Saying "Be a Big Kid"**
  Children will try to do their best. Added pressure or embarrassment does not help. It is harmful for the child to develop negative feelings about himself.

- ☐ **Making Promises You May Not Be Able to Keep**
  Additional disappointments will only add to a child's sense of frustration.

- ☐ **Talking About Children As If They Are Not There**
  Children hear and understand more than we think. Misconceptions and fears may arise from fragments of information that were overheard and not explained.

- ☐ **Asking Children Why They Are in the Hospital**
  Questions of this nature should not be a part of casual conversation. Children may not be comfortable discussing something so personal.

- ☐ **Talking in a Negative Manner**
  Try to state things in a positive manner. Inform children of what they can do instead of what they cannot do.

- ☐ **Losing Your Self Control**
  If you find you are losing your patience seek someone else to work with the child.

This attractive two-color, 11" x 17" poster is available from: Child Life Council of ACCH
7910 Woodmont Ave., #300, Bethesda, MD 20814
Adapted from: Cleveland Clinic Foundation

Child Life Council

Volunteers in Child Health:

Orientation and Training Resources

Some Helpful Techniques in Managing Children's Behavior

Do:

Listen actively and with respect.
- Whether the message is verbal or non-verbal, you can listen carefully and reflect back the feeling you hear expressed.

Give all directions in the positive.
- Tell the child that he can do. "You can walk to the playroom." ... "I want you to lie down now."

Pay attention to good behaviors.
- Acknowledge the behaviors you want to be continued. "You do a great job of picking up your toys." ... "The way you hold still helped me so much!"

Ignore negative behavior.
- Whenever possible, ignore those little attention-getting behaviors. If you do respond, make sure it is in a calm way.

Involve the child in solving problems.
- When you have a conflict, let the child know how you see the problem, listen to her response, and work out a mutually agreeable solution, especially with teens.

Use language geared to the child's developmental level.
- Consider the vocabulary you choose as well as the complexity. Remember your non-verbal resources.

Don't:

Use intimidating, threatening, preaching, and judging statement, such as:
- "If you don't cooperate, we'll have to call your doctor/mother."
- "You're a big boy now, you don't need to cry."
- "You are being such a grouch today. Just cheer up."

Ask questions when you intend to give directions.
- "Would you like to get your bath now?"
- "It's time to check your I.V., okay?"

Adapted from: Child Life Department, Columbus Children's Hospital, Columbus, Ohio.

Management, Selection, Training & Supervision

Appendix B

Limits and Limit Setting

CHILDREN NEED LIMITS, as do all people. Children need to know how they are expected to behave. They are happier and more secure when they know that the adults who are caring for them are not going to let them get out of bounds. They are grateful to the adult who is firm in seeing that they stay within reasonable limits. Limits should be based on the needs of the individual, the group, physical dangers, and the total situation. Guidance must be appropriate as well as consistent.

Illness presents many problems for the child, the family, and for those caring for the child in health settings. We need to remind ourselves, constantly, that the patient is first of all a child, and, insofar, as possible, needs to be treated like other children his or her age, while still considering any special needs caused by illness or disability.

Setting limits is not simple and it is impossible to make rules that apply to every child and all situations. During illness and especially when a child is away from home, our responsibility is to give the child the security of limits maintained by stable adults who want to help him or her to continue to grow towards maturity and self control.

A Child Must Be Stopped If He Or She Is:

1. Hurting self.
2. Hurting others (physically or emotionally).
3. Destroying equipment.
4. Over-stimulated to the point of losing self control.

Avoid:

1. Using such words as "bad" or "not nice".
2. Using threats or bribes.
3. Punishing because of your anger.
4. Giving punishment that has no relationship to the misdeed.

Do:

1. Try to establish good rapport as soon as possible.
2. Redirecting a child is likely to be most effective when it is consistent with the child's own motives or interest. Teach the child a desirable response, do not just control the situation.
3. When limits are necessary, they should be clearly defined and consistently maintained.

Adapted from: Volunteer Manual, Child Life Department, The Johns Hopkins Children's Center, Baltimore, MD.

What Will You Say Or Do?

Volunteers can practice responding to some common situations in advance. The following situations are used as role plays in volunteer training. Individual volunteers can also think through their responses and discuss each situation with a supervisor.

1. Introduce yourself to a child and invite to the playroom.
2. Two children are fighting over a toy.
3. A child is crying because mom had to leave, and the child is too sick to come to the playroom.
4. You go into a room, but the child refuses to give you a verbal response.
5. You're in the middle of a game with a child in their room and the mother returns and asks you to leave. What to you say/do?
6. You observe "inappropriate" parent-child interaction.
7. A child lashes out and directs a temper tantrum at you.
8. Your supervisor is out sick or on vacation.
9. A child asks you to bring them candy/present on your next visit.
10. You promised a child you would play a game but you are out of time. What are your responsibilities to yourself, the unit and the child?
11. How do you know what an IV is beeping about? What do you do?
12. You see blood, a child vomiting, a child choking. What should you do?
13. You are involved in an accident with a child. What should you do?
14. Your supervisor does not have time to talk and never seems to give feedback.
15. Two children get into a "physical" fight.
16. A child has a significant abnormality/injury. How do you get around staring? Is it okay to look? What if a child asks out loud about the "injured" child's problems?
17. A parent asks you "What's wrong with that patient?", "Why doesn't his mother/father visit?"

Adapted from: Child Life Department the John Hopkins Children's Center Baltimore, Maryland

Appendix B

Medical Play

The purposes of medical play are:

1. To acquaint children with materials and equipment that are potentially stress-inducing in a relaxed, comfortable environment. To provide preparation for events the child will experience.

2. To provide the child an opportunity to express anger, rage, revenge, hostility, resentment, sadness, etc., within an acceptable, controlled framework with the support and presence of an adult.

3. To provide an opportunity for the child to work through a "blocking" of feelings such as anger so that the feelings become openly expressed rather than a repressive, interfering agent in the child's ability to interact with his or her environment in ways more typical of the child prior to the hospital experience.

4. To provide an opportunity for the child to interact with other children in medical play, thereby opening up a means for shared communication of feelings.

5. To provide an opportunity for the supervising adult to reality-base the child's fantasy, impart factual, specific information about medical events and impart information about expectations for desired behaviors of the child held by the care givers.

6. To provide an opportunity for the supervising adult to observe the child, thereby gaining insight into the child's understanding and coping processes with a specific procedure, illness, or the more general stress of hospitalization.

The procedures to be followed are:

1. Medical play must always be directly supervised.

2. As many, or as few, children as the supervising adult can comfortably control may be involved in the play.

3. The recipient of the medical play procedures must always be a fantasy object (stuffed animal or doll, etc.) never a real person (adult or child.) Acceptable social behavior does not include physically harming another person. To include real people as recipients or fantasy material dealing with body harm and intrusion as an expression of anger can be confusing for the child. In order to maintain the child's comfortably handling angry expressions it is necessary that the child be limited to fantasy objects as recipients of fantasy material of medical play.

If a child wants to give a real person "an injection, a shot", the supervising adult must interject by saying . . . "John, Susan is a real person and only doctors and nurses give injections to real people in our hospital. Real people don't get play shots; they only get shots, injections when they need to have medicine. Since you are playing the doctor, let 'bear' play the patient and I'll play like I'm talking for him."

4. Only one needle should be in use regardless of the number of children involved in the play. The supervising adult must always know where the needle is. If for any reason the supervising adult has to move away from the children, no matter how briefly, the needle must be taken with the adult.

5. At the conclusion of the play, the needle must immediately be returned to the closet shelf where it is kept.

6. Materials used in medical play are found in the storeroom or playroom closets.

Materials are stored by type (all masks are in one container, etc. Take out what you need. Return items to their correct box.)

Materials to include:

- Fantasy objects — dolls, stuffed animals, etc.
- Puppets — doctor, nurse, family, animals
- Medical equipment — stethoscopes, band-aids, tape, gauze, IV set-up, arm board, blood pressure cuff, surgical hats, masks, gloves
- Hospital play furniture

Particular behaviors to watch for and channel in more appropriate manner:

1. Aggression spilling over from play and fantasy object to other children — The child caught up in the fantasy can begin to lose control of the feeling being expressed, particularly aggression. To help the child gain control: touch the child on the shoulder, arm, or knee — if sitting. Your hand should remain there until you are sure the child is in control. This action on your part is calming and helps focus the child's attention on you so he or she can attend to your words. "Janey, you are talking loud. I feel uncomfortable when you talk so loud. Remember, Bear is the patient — Can you hear him talk if you talk loud? Listen. What's he saying?"Doctor, you hurt me. Do you like to hurt me?" The child's response to the question then provides cues as to how to continue to focus the child's attention on the play and fantasy object so that the focus is maintained, not lost to the child's loss of control.

2. Withdrawal — A child initially appearing eager or somewhat eager to play but withdrawing verbally and/or nonverbally as play proceeds may be feeling very threatened. The play may be arousing a great deal of fear and feelings of vulnerability. The child should be allowed to discontinue the play with comforting remarks such as: "Susan, you seem quiet now. I think you don't like this play right now. Does it seem kind of scary? You know lots of children get scared in the hospital sometimes but this is just play. It's not going to happen to you right now. If you want to, you don't have to do this doctor play. You can go paint at the table (or whatever activity is appropriate)." Remember this child. Continue to develop a trusting, non-threatening, non-demanding relationship with her. When she feels secure with you, reintroduce the medical play in a one-to-one setting at first.

Take it slowly. Be very aware of her body language. But be sure she eventually is able to play out these feelings that are blocking her play.

3. Denial — Example: "Shots don't hurt." Some children may unrealistically deny feelings of pain and hurt. It is important that they hear the message that we accept expressions of feeling without putting down their particular defense. "Amy, you looked kind of proud when you said shots don't hurt you. I think it must feel good to you to know that you can take an injection when you have to. You know, some kids who have to have injections don't like them. They think they hurt some, and they may cry. It's o.k. if they cry when it does hurt, and its great when they can hold real still. I wonder what Bear will do when he has a shot?" Then play out on Bear for Amy to have an opportunity to play out crying.

4. Location of procedure — Some children will vary the location of the procedure given to the fantasy object's body. Other children will choose one consistent location. Be aware of this. Remember the child and consistent location. Mention this to the staff. It may be that this represents the one kind of procedure the child finds most upsetting. Example: Always the arm could mean blood drawing. Always the middle of the back could mean lumbar punctures.

If the child consistently chooses one or a variety of unusual places — shots in the eyes, stomach, genital area — this may be an expression of the child's fantasy — the fear of what may be attacked. Allow the child to play out the procedure, but again notify the staff so that this child can be followed up in additional medical play sessions. It could be that the child has had an unusual procedure or surgery on a particular part of the body. This too can be followed up with factual information as the child plays — explanations about the surgery, why the child had to have it, etc. Again, check with the staff to clarify.

Source: Sally Francis, Director, Child Life Program, Children's Medical Center of Dallas, TX

Exercise: The Habit of Reflection

Volunteering with people is never a static experience. For volunteers who are alert and sensitive, each situation presents an opportunity for service and personal growth. How can volunteers remain open to new experiences?

Take time to reflect on your experiences at the end of each day. Some guiding questions which can assist you in this review process are:

1. What happened today?

2. What was the best thing that happened?

3. Why did this seem good?

4. What was going on?

5. Did I learn something which can be applied to similar situations?

6. Were there any not-so-good moments?

7. What was going on?

8. What seemed to be the cause? Could I be wrong in my assessment?

9. Is there anything else I need to know?

10. Could this have been prevented?

(Continued)

11. Is there anything I need to follow-up on?

12. Is there anything I should discuss with a staff person?

13. Have I learned anything about myself.

14. What will I do differently next time?

Sharing Significant Observations

VOLUNTEERS ARE THE EXTRA HANDS, eyes, ears, and hearts of the child health care service. Frequently it is a sensitive volunteer who is the first to notice when something doesn't seem quite right. It may be a subtle change in a child's appearance, an unusual noise from a piece of equipment, or a clear sign that a child, parent, or visitor seems quite upset. Volunteers need to trust their instincts, and not hesitate to follow through appropriately with concerns.

Volunteers increase their abilities to provide direct support through experience. However, as skills increase, so does the ability to note subtle changes earlier. **A good general rule to follow is: always share your concerns and observations with staff before you leave.** Do not decide that you are probably wrong, or that your observation is too insignificant to be important. Staff is not too busy to be bothered. Staff members appreciate having alert sensitive volunteers. Your observations are important.

Source: Arlene Kiely, Training Consultant, ACCH, Bethesda, MD

Self Evaluation and Action Plan

1. What else do I need to know to help me do the best possible job as a volunteer?

2. What resources will I need to help me become better prepared?

3. What action will I take?

By (Date)

I will:

Source: Arlene Kiely, Training Consultant, ACCH, Bethesda, MD

Appendix C: Evaluation of Publication

Appendix C

Volunteers in Child Health: Management, Selection, Training & Supervision

ACCH invites your help in evaluating the usefulness of this publication. Please complete and return this form. Please feel free to add extra pages for more extensive responses, and to photocopy this form for each individual who wishes to respond. Thank you for taking the time to share your response.

1. Please check your overall rating of the content and organization of the publication:

    Content:

    ❑ Poor ❑ Fair ❑ Good ❑ Excellent

    Organization:

    ❑ Poor ❑ Fair ❑ Good ❑ Excellent

2. Check ways you have used or will use this manual:
    - ❑ reference
    - ❑ to train staff
    - ❑ handouts for volunteers
    - ❑ educate other agency personnel
    - ❑ develop orientation outline
    - ❑ develop training manual
    - ❑ improve supervision
    - ❑ other

3. Please rate the overall helpfulness of each section used:

	not used	poor	fair	very good	good	outstanding
Section I: Administration and Management						
Section II: Training						
Section III: Supervision						
Appendix A: Management Resources						
Appendix B: Training Resources						

Evaluation of Publication

4. Rate the overall usefulness for the following persons in your agency:

	not used	poor	fair	very good	good	outstanding
volunteer coordinator						
trainers of volunteers						
staff members						
supervisors						
volunteers						
administrators						
others:						

5. What specific sections or materials are most helpful for staff, and why?

6. What materials are most helpful to volunteers, and why?

7. What information covered issues not previously addressed in your setting?

8. Please describe any changes or improvements you have made as a result of this manual:

Appendix C

9. What information or materials would you add?

10. Would you recommend this manual for others? If so, for what kinds of settings?

11. How did you learn about this manual?

12. Do you feel this manual is worth the cost? ❏ yes ❏ no

13. Please indicate the following:
    Your profession or role:
    Type of agency:
    Type of community: ❏ Large metropolitan ❏ Urban ❏ Small town ❏ Rural

14. Please add any other comments or information you wish:

Thank you for sharing your evaluation with us.

Please return to:
ACCH Publication Center
7910 Woodmont Avenue, Suite 300
Bethesda, MD 20814

NOTES

NOTES